ELIJAH,
PROPHET OF GOD

by
LEON J. WOOD, PH.D.
Dean of the Seminary and Professor of Old Testament Studies
Grand Rapids Baptist Bible College and Seminary

WIPF & STOCK · Eugene, Oregon

Wipf and Stock Publishers
199 W 8th Ave, Suite 3
Eugene, OR 97401

Elijah
Prophet of God
By Wood, Leon J.
Copyright©1968 by Wood, Leon J.
ISBN 13: 978-1-60608-586-8
Publication date 4/2/2009
Previously published by Regular Baptist Press, 1968

TO MY WIFE AND FAMILY

TABLE OF CONTENTS

PREFACE

Biographies of great people stimulate the readers to set higher goals in their own lives. This is especially true concerning biographies of persons in the Bible. Though we do not find any complete records of lives portrayed there, considerable information is given regarding many, and what there is may be taken as particularly significant to account for this inclusion.

This Biblical biography forms an important part to sacred history. Sacred history is unique in that not only man's activities on earth are related but also the nature of God's reaction to them in Heaven. When people conduct themselves correctly, God shows approval through blessing; when they do not, hardship and trouble are experienced. This provides both principle and illustration for our learning as to what manner of conduct, in a host of life-situations, is pleasing to God and what is not. In this there is great practical benefit for Christian living.

With these thoughts in mind, the study of Elijah contained in these pages has been undertaken. The intention has been to examine the meaning of all parts of the story; to probe implications as to mental attitudes, desires, emotional reactions and the general character of Elijah and other persons involved; and to observe theological and practical significances both for that day and now.

Appreciation is here extended to Dr. Warren H. Faber, a colleague at the Grand Rapids Baptist Bible College and Seminary, for reading the complete manuscript and making helpful suggestions. The text employed in quotations from the Bible is the American Standard Version.

LEON J. WOOD

Chapter One

RELIGIOUS DARKNESS

Elijah is uniquely important among God's servants. Scripture indicates this in unusual ways. In all history, only two men were permitted to bypass death—Enoch and Elijah. Two men were privileged to appear with Christ on the Mount of Transfiguration—Moses and Elijah. And Malachi predicted that Elijah would return before "the great and terrible day of Jehovah" (Mal. 4:5), with the result that people in Jesus' day, anticipating Elijah's reappearance, identified Jesus as Elijah (Mark 8:28).

Background

Elijah lived in a day when the northern kingdom of Israel had grown strong but was filled with gross spiritual darkness. Ahab, son of the ambitious and capable Omri, was king. Israel had not been strong before Omri came to the throne, but he did much to make it so. He first defeated a rival, Tibni (1 Kings 16:22), and then built the strong capital city, Samaria (1 Kings 16:23, 24). He defeated and laid heavy tribute upon neighboring Moab across the Jordan,[1] and Assyrian notices show that his fame spread to other distant countries.[2]

Ahab sought to follow in his father's footsteps and showed considerable ability in military matters, construction activity and statesmanship. Syria, recently risen to a power position in the north, was defeated twice (1 Kings 20:1-34). He joined a coalition of twelve kings at Karkar to stop the advancing Shalmaneser III of Assyria, and was able to supply more chariots than any of the other eleven.[3] First Kings 22:39 says that he built several cities, as well as an ivory palace for himself. His marriage to Jezebel was clearly part of a diplomatic alliance with the prosperous maritime neighbor, Phoenicia. Treaties of this kind, cemented by marriages, were common to the day. That Ahab had the foresight and capacity to negotiate an agreement of this kind, which probably proved of real economic benefit, testifies to his ability as a statesman.

But the story is different in respect to religion. Whatever commendation is due him in other ways, it is quite lost to sight in the darkness of his spiritual deficiency. First Kings 16:30 states, "And Ahab the son of Omri did that which was evil in the sight of Jehovah *above all* that were before him" (italics mine). The reason cited is that he not only continued the God-displeasing practices of his predecessors, but he "went and served Baal, and worshipped him" (v. 31).

The practices of the former kings had already seriously broken with the law. Jeroboam, Israel's first ruler following the kingdom division, had started it.[4] He had feared that his people would turn their allegiance back to Jerusalem if they should continue worshiping at the temple there, and so had made substitute centers of worship at Dan and Bethel in his own country. In each city he placed a golden image of a calf as a symbol for the new program. He ordained priests from other than Levites and erected altars for sacrifice. All this soon called for rebuke, and a "man of God" was sent for the purpose (1 Kings 13:1-6). But Jeroboam persisted, and his successors followed suit.

Thus it was when Ahab came to the throne; but then he added that which was worse—Baal worship. The former worship, deficient as it was, was still a worship of Jehovah.[5]

This, however, brought in a substitute god, Baal. It also brought extreme moral degradation as its official accompaniment.

Entrance of Baal Worship

Baal worship was not new to Israel. It had been widely followed in premonarchial days. It had been the religion of the Canaanites before the conquest and many Israelites had been influenced by them upon entering the land. Baal was supposed to be the god of rain and good crops. The Canaanites believed that one must worship Baal to prosper as a farmer. Israel, fresh from desert life, had to learn agricultural ways upon reaching the new land.[6] The people listened to the former inhabitants and were told that worshiping Baal was the most important feature. Many followed the advice. In fact, in the region of Abiezer[7] adherence to Baal became so strong that Gideon's neighbors wished to take his life for daring to destroy their local Baal altar (Judg. 6:30). God, knowing beforehand these dangers, had warned Israel to drive the former inhabitants out, but Israel had not obeyed.

Finally, Baal worship had been all but exterminated, especially during the reign of David.[8] The blessing of God during this time and that of Solomon must be attributed in large part to this fact. Then, under Ahab, it returned. The marriage with Jezebel brought it about. Probably Ahab had thought of this marriage, at the time, as only a diplomatic nicety, but it proved to be his greatest mistake. The Phoenician alliance had seemed a brilliant stroke of diplomacy; but, in this marriage, it developed as the cause of his downfall. Jezebel was strong-willed and intent on bringing her religion with her to the new country.

There is evidence that this introduction of Baal worship was far more her idea than Ahab's, although he gave acquiescence when he should have resisted, and so is chargeable with blame (1 Kings 16:31). But he did not inaugurate the idea and may have been unhappy that she did.

One factor indicating this is that Jezebel had the personality to force such a matter even though her husband disapproved. In a day when women ordinarily were little heard, she even issued orders in her own name. She sent a threatening note to Elijah following the Mount Carmel contest which prompted him to flee (1 Kings 19:2, 3), and at a later time perpetrated the vicious plot to obtain Ahab's coveted vineyard from Naboth (1 Kings 21:1-16). Another factor is that the leadership in the Baal program is ascribed to Jezebel, but never to Ahab. The Baal prophets are called those "that eat at Jezebel's table" (1 Kings 18:19), and she was also the one who ordered the killing of Jehovah's prophets (1 Kings 18:4). A third factor is that when Ahab himself wanted divine counsel, he looked to the prophets of Jehovah, not those of Baal. This was demonstrated prior to the Ramoth-gilead battle when Jehoshaphat of Judah was with him (1 Kings 22).[9]

In view of these thoughts, a practical note is suggested. Marriages are extremely important. They are often taken too lightly. Marriage partners are selected without careful consideration, and the ceremony is performed before real acquaintance is made. But marriage is a life decision. So much difference can result in accordance with the choice of a partner. Good men have been broken because of unsuited wives, as indeed have good wives because of unsuited husbands. Ahab would have been a far better man and ruler had he not married this scheming, ambitious, heathen princess. His own life was sadly affected as well as the course of the entire country. The marriage state should not be entered lightly or quickly because it is one of the most important steps in life.

Character and Extent of Baal Worship

The character of Baal worship is well-known, especially from the epic literature of Ras Shamra.[10] Baal was the son of El. He was thought to give increase to family, flocks and crops. Accordingly, fertility rites played a large part in his worship. Licentious dances were prominent, and chambers existed for both male and female prostitutes. Animal sacrifices were included in the ritual, which was observed either in grand temples or outdoor areas called "high places." A main Baal altar was normally accompanied by the "Asherah" pole carved in honor of the goddess of that name, the consort of Baal.[11]

Several matters testify to the extensive inroad this religion made into Israel under Jezebel's insistence. One is that Elijah stood alone on Mount Carmel in contest with four hundred and fifty representatives of Baal, and said that he was the only prophet of Jehovah remaining (1 Kings 18:22). Another comes from Elijah's despairing statement on Mount Horeb a few days later that he was the only one left in all Israel who worshiped Jehovah. God corrected him, saying that actually there were seven thousand, but how few this number in an entire nation! A third is that Jezebel dared to take the extreme step of slaying Jehovah prophets when she was the foreigner and they the native clergy.[12] And a fourth is that Baal worship was able to continue strong through at least the reigns of Ahab's two sons and was still flourishing when Jehu came to the throne.[13]

From this it is clear that by the time of the Mount Carmel contest, Baal worship had all but blotted out the worship of Jehovah. In fact, after the slaying of the Jehovah prophets, it is likely that no formal observance of the former religion continued.[14] What few persons maintained allegiance to Jehovah had to do so in secret. Baal worship had become the official religion of the land.

Footnotes to Chapter One:

¹Indicated on the Moabite Stone, written by Mesha, king of Moab, contemporary with Jehoram (cf. 2 Kings 3:4). For description and text, cf. W. H. Bennett, "Moab, Moabites," *HDB,* III, pp. 402-413.

²For instance, Adad-nirari III (810-782 B.C.), living three-quarters of a century later, refers to Israel as "the land of Omri." Cf. G. A. Barton, *Archaeology and the Bible* (7th ed.; Philadelphia: American Sunday School Union, 1937), pp. 462, 463.

³He supplied two thousand. For listing of all allies with the contributions, cf. text of Shalmaneser in G. A. Barton, *ibid.,* pp. 457, 458.

⁴First Kings 12:25-33.

⁵Indicated by the lack of any other deity being named in connection with it; also by Jeroboam's evident tying this worship to the earlier infraction in the wilderness which was a worship of Jehovah as indicated specifically by Aaron (1 Kings 12:28; Exod. 32:4, 5). W. F. Albright suggests that Jeroboam desired the people to think of Jehovah as standing invisibly on the backs of these calves. Cf. *From the Stone Age to Christianity* (2nd ed.; Baltimore: Johns Hopkins Press, 1946), p. 229.

⁶Israel had not farmed in the desert, being fed by the Manna; and those who had worked the land in Egypt had died, except Caleb and Joshua. Moreover, farming methods differed in Egypt, which was watered by the "foot" (cf. Deut. 11:10, 11) in irrigation, while Palestine depended on rainfall.

⁷Tribe of Manasseh likely somewhere in the valley of Esdraelon.

⁸In the time of Rehoboam of Judah, some mention is made of high places, an Asherah pole and Sodomites, which shows that Baal worship in a degree yet remained, or even had been reintroduced (1 Kings 14:21-24).

⁹It is further significant that Ahab's children, Ahaziah, Jehoram and Athaliah, all bore names reflecting Jehovah's name and not Baal's. They were born before Baal worship reached its strength in Israel, but Ahab's own sympathies are reflected in the official names bestowed.

¹⁰Ras Shamra, called Ugarit in ancient times, is located on the Syrian coast near the Orontes River. Discoveries there have been called some of the most significant in Near Eastern archaeology. The city was destroyed about 1200 B.C.

¹¹For example, Gideon was directed both to destroy the Baal altar and cut down the Asherah pole, which was to be used for fuel on the new Jehovah altar (Judg. 6:25-27).

¹² First Kings 18:4. One does not lightly put his hand on native clergy, especially when he is himself a foreigner. Few things bring

greater resentment. Jezebel must have believed her position very secure to chance this move.

[13]Jehu gathered the Baal prophets into their temple and slaughtered them there (2 Kings 10:19-28).

[14]Cessation of the worship was certainly Jezebel's main objective in this move.

Chapter Two

ELIJAH BEFORE AHAB

Little information is given about Elijah as he steps upon the scene in 1 Kings 17:1. His name, Elijah the Tishbite, is mentioned and the region where he lived, Gilead. Nothing, however, is included as to parentage, education or general background. In fact, the reader tends to look back to prior chapters to see if he could have been introduced before, but nothing is there.

There *is* significance in the little information given. His name, Elijah, means, "My God is Jehovah." Godly parents come to mind as those who would bestow it. "The Tishbite" probably refers to his birthplace. A town bearing the name "Tishbe" was located in northern Galilee.[1] However, since Gilead is said to have been his home country, he must have soon moved if the Galilean location first housed his young life. Gilead, east of the Jordan, was thought of as backward in culture. Elijah, described as "a hairy man, and girt with a girdle of leather about his loins" (2 Kings 1:8), was likely thought of as a true product of the region. Backward though it was, Gilead was also away from the decadent religious centers of the day, and so the young Elijah would have been sheltered from their influence. Even the cultural lack itself could have played a part in developing his rugged individualism. It is hardship, not ease, which best molds true strength and character.

A significant note regarding Elijah prior to his introduction in 1 Kings 17:1 is given in James 5:17: "Elijah was a man of like passions with us, and he prayed fervently that it might not rain; and it rained not on the earth for three years and six months." This prayer did precede the 1 Kings 17:1 introduction,[2] for it only requested what Elijah then told the king would happen.

Two matters regarding the prayer, both highly commendable to the prophet, should be noticed. One is that he was a man mighty in prayer. The request given was enormous: rainfall should cease! And it was granted. This was true, effective praying; it is the point, in fact, which James illustrates in citing it. The other is that Elijah was keenly conscious of sin. It was his consciousness of the great sin of the day that prompted the prayer. God had long before warned that famine would be an occasional method to bring reprimand,[3] and Elijah was asking Him to employ it. He would not have requested this lightly, which stresses the degree of the burden he felt.

Are any characteristics more important in the life of God's servants than these two—mighty in prayer and keenly conscious of sin? Both are rare. It is easy to pray mechanically; not truly and effectively. Accordingly, seldom are concrete answers of this kind seen. How callous we become toward sin! We see it commonly and tend to excuse it. But God does not. Neither did Elijah. We need more Elijahs today in God's work.

Appearance Before Ahab

The reason for Elijah's appearance before Ahab follows logically in view of the request he made. God heard it, indicated His affirmative answer, and then gave Elijah the assignment of telling the king. If the famine was to accomplish its purpose, the king must know who was to send it and why. Only then would he and the people profit from its lessons. Elijah, who had cared enough to pray, was also best suited to

17

convey the message. How often God sends the same person who prays to carry out the request given! The faith that prompts the prayer can also give the needed implementation. We can only guess as to how God arranged for Elijah to make his entrance before the king. Crude of dress and likely of speech, the prophet would have been denied official audience. This means it must have been unofficial. Perhaps it was timed when Ahab was at his alternate palace in Jezreel,[4] where precautions would have been less. The king may have been walking unattended in the palace grounds, with a gate left open. He may even have been thinking of his domineering wife, her unanticipated hold on the land, and the rising power of the Baal priests. This would have set the stage nicely for Elijah's entrance and message. God's servants are not limited merely to natural developments when doing His work. When there is need for supernatural intervention, He provides it in just such a way as this.

Message, First Half

Elijah's message to Ahab was brief, but weighty. No doubt he had memorized every word. It could not be long, with the visit unannounced and the words so serious. Guards might be summoned quickly.

Although brief, the message carried two parts. The first was introductory and in the form of an oath: "As Jehovah, the God of Israel, liveth, before whom I stand" (1 Kings 17:1). Oaths were common.[5] They added notes of seriousness or solemnity to statements or occasions of unusual importance. Different forms were used. A common one was, "God do so and more also; for . . ." (e.g. 1 Sam. 14:44). Another was, "As Jehovah liveth" (e.g. 1 Sam. 14:39), which was a part of the form employed here. The longer form here was peculiarly Elijah's own. He used it one other time (1 Kings 18:15) and Elisha, who learned from him, used it twice (2 Kings 3:14; 5:16). Perhaps the prophet had framed

18

it in view of the sin of the day, since it carries great significance in respect to it.[6] It was far more than merely a form of convenience and calls for close attention.

Three main thoughts are involved. The first comes in the opening words, "As Jehovah, the God of Israel." Elijah was calling attention to the basic wrong in the kingdom; indeed, the reason why he had come to Ahab. Jehovah was Israel's God, not Baal. The king had been wrong in permitting Baal to enter. This was the reason for the dire message he was bringing. Plainly, Elijah did not start by talking of things in general. He went directly to the heart of that which was wrong in the land.

The second is in the word "liveth." "As Jehovah, the God of Israel, liveth." This brought challenge to Baal, for the implication was that he did not. Jehovah lives: He is the true God, the only living God!

The third is the courageous declaration, "Before whom I stand." This was Elijah's way of identifying which side he was on: Jehovah's, not Baal's. The form used would have been easily understood by Ahab. The expression was taken from the court: those who attended kings were those who "stood before them."[7] Elijah stood before Jehovah. He was Jehovah's servant. Ahab should be clear on this point when the rainless weeks would begin.

It took great courage to make this uncompromising declaration. Remember that Baal worship had now become the state religion. Jezebel had not yet taken the extreme step of slaying Jehovah prophets, but the conditions which made it possible were rapidly becoming existent. It was already unpopular, if not dangerous, to admit preference for Jehovah publicly.[8] Yet, Elijah was at the palace, talking to the king himself and announcing his unequivocal allegiance to Jehovah, the true and rightful God of Israel! Need it be said that God desires the same fearless conviction today? Elijah did not seem to care for his own welfare; he was performing God's assignment.

Message, Second Half

The second part was the message proper. He said, "There shall not be dew nor rain these years, but according to my word." Again, three thoughts are evident.

The first is, "There shall not be dew nor rain." Here was grave warning. Water was of the utmost importance. The land prospered in the measure that rain fell. Elijah was saying that there would be no rain at all. No message could have been more serious in the ears of the king. We may assume, too, that God timed this announcement most advantageously; that is, at that season of the year when rain was most expected. The dry season lasts from May to October.[9] If Elijah had given this announcement in the spring or summer, it would have been forgotten by the time the normal rains failed to appear. God would have wanted it given in October, just before the rains were expected, and at the close of the annual six-month drought which made everyone look longingly for them.[10]

The second thought is in the words "these years." These two words added further seriousness to the message. The country would suffer enough if the expected rain did not come for a few weeks, but Elijah was speaking of "these years." This meant not only the early rains then anticipated, but the heavier winter rains, and then the latter spring rains; and all this not only for one season, but at least two. Actually, as we know, it was to last for three and one-half years, which means four full seasons.[11] This spelled catastrophe of the worst kind to Ahab. Little of which he could think would harm his country as much.

The third suggestion is stated in the phrase, "but according to my word." This tragic condition would continue until Elijah gave the word for change. He, Jehovah's prophet, would control the duration. There was nothing the king could do to change it.

Few messages could have been so disturbing and shocking as this. Without rain wells dry up; food does not grow; suffering becomes intense; people starve and die. Elijah knew the weight of his words. He had lived near the desert all his life. But he also knew the sinful character of Baal worship and the tenacity with which people hold to their sin. More than light measures would be needed. God's own prescribed method of famine would alone strike hard enough to check the onrush of this Jehovah-defying movement.

Again the courage of Elijah stands out. He dared to bring a message of this kind to the king. Kings like prosperous conditions. They want contentment for their people. But Elijah was predicting famine, which meant the worst of trouble. Eiljah knew the effect these words might have on the king, but still he spoke them. There could be great danger for him, but God had given the task. He was in God's hands and God would protect him if this was His will. There is great peace in simple resignation to God's will. In this should be life's central motivation. Then, whether God protects so that one lives, or withholds that protection so that one dies, still all is well. This is what Paul had in mind when he wrote, "For to me to live is Christ, and to die is gain" (Phil. 1:21).

Elijah's faith as displayed here is equally exemplary. He was asserting that he would control rainfall. He, as Jehovah's prophet, would both keep it from raining and give the word when it could start again. This took great faith. In few situations does man normally feel as helpless as before the power of nature. Who would attempt to stop a storm in its fury? Or who would try to make rain clouds in an empty, blue sky? Without question, Ahab thought Elijah quite demented for such a claim. No one in his right mind would make it. But Elijah did because God had said so, and he believed.

Reasons for the Message

One reason prompting this message has been noticed. The famine would be a way to call the people from their sin. It would have been effective to that end, too. Even though the people may have forgotten God's specific warning through Moses, their own consciences would have told them that this was a visitation from God. Jehovah was speaking in wrath because Baal was being made to replace Him in Israel. This recognition would have been reaffirmed by Ahab's own search for Elijah, soon to be conducted.[12] He would seek him as Jehovah's prophet who had sent the famine.

There was also a second reason. It was that God was hereby challenging Baal's power and existence. Baal was supposed to be the god of rain and good crops. His specialty was making farmers prosperous. So for Jehovah to proclaim that it would not rain, until His prophet gave the word, was to challenge Baal's central domain. In other words, a contest was being instituted.[13] Who was the greater, Jehovah or Baal? Could Baal make it rain when Jehovah said it would not? Elijah had used the word "liveth" for Jehovah. By this contest this claim would be proved: Jehovah liveth, but Baal does not.

How was the contest to develop? What would happen in the ensuing months to make its existence and significance known? We may safely conjecture. At first, Ahab would have paid little attention to Elijah's words. Certainly this strange fellow need not be taken seriously. But as rainless days and weeks passed, with complaints coming daily to the palace, Ahab would become serious. Could there be something to what this crude fellow had said after all? But his mind would have yet resisted this possibility and turned rather to the Baal prophets. They were supposed to be expert in rain-making. Let Jezebel show, now when it really counted, what they could do. And Jezebel would have been glad to do so. It not only would please the king, but now, when people needed rain so badly, it would prove the value of the Baal program as never before. She would have given the orders and the prophets would have done their best. However, as we know, their best would not be good enough. Rain did not fall. Jezebel would then have become angry and perhaps she would have employed extreme measures, such as changing personnel or even taking lives, yet without result.

This situation would have lasted for a few weeks, but in time Ahab's patience would have run out. Conditions were becoming more desperate daily. Rain must be made to fall. His mind would have turned once more to the peculiar prophet. Humiliating to admit, it must be that his words were responsible. So let him be found. From 1 Kings 18:10 we know that he sent messengers all over the land and even to surrounding nations. As they went, the all-important facts would have become known: Jehovah's prophet had said that it would not rain; Baal's prophets apparently were not able to make it rain. In this way all would have learned of the contest situation. Jehovah was being proved the more powerful by withholding the rain in opposition to Baal. Jehovah was greater than Baal.

In this double intention behind Elijah's message, we see again the all-comprehending wisdom of God. Who would think that one short message could accomplish so much? It was the opening move in forty-two months of preparations for revival. The climax was to come with the great contest for fire on Mount Carmel, but in anticipation the people needed to be preconditioned. They needed to be rebuked for their sin, and they needed to be shown in a persistent, continuous manner that Jehovah was superior to Baal. To start it off, Elijah's message to the king was necessary. By it both king and people would be made to know the significance of what God was doing.

We do well to remind ourselves often of the greatness of God's wisdom. We know of it in general terms, but somehow its reality does not penetrate the way we live and think. We even have a tendency to question His plans at times ourselves, as though there could be any room for improvement. We have a sample in this message, however, of how superior His wisdom is. No man would or could have planned it this way. Elijah may have hesitated at first to give it, for real danger was involved. But he did not stop. He obeyed, believing God knew best. Again he provides an excellent example. We should do the same.

Footnotes to Chapter Two:

[1]Mentioned in Tobias 1:2.

[2]James also refers to Elijah's prayer for rain, the record of which is given (1 Kings 18:42-44), as likewise an example of effective praying.

[3]Deuteronomy 11:17; 28:23; cf. 1 Kings 8:35.

[4]Ahab and Jezebel seem to have spent as much time at Jezreel as at Samaria. Cf. 1 Kings 18:46; 21:1.

[5]Oaths were of different types and used to signify different things. Cf. "Oath," *Unger's Bible Dictionary*, pp. 800, 801.

[6]Each time of its employment, the circumstances called for just the significance it carried.

[7]Cf., for example, 1 Kings 10:8: "Happy are thy men, happy are these thy servants, that *stand continually before thee*" (italics mine). Cf. also 1 Kings 12:6, 8; 2 Chron. 29:11.

[8]For Jezebel to have held the control she did, particularly at the time of slaying the Jehovah prophets, she must have had informants throughout the land, which fact would have been known and feared. Her ruthless character is illustrated in her treatment of these prophets and also Naboth.

[9]Israel experiences six months dry season and six months wet. The early rains start in October and are important for they are so desired after the long summer. The winter rains are the heaviest, and the latter rains usually come to an end during April and are lighter again. They are important for people know that when they end, the dry season follows.

[10]With the drought lasting three and a half years, the rain again started when otherwise not expected. That is, three and a half years would have brought the time to the middle of April when the latter rains should stop. Thus God started withholding rain when it should have begun, and gave rain when it should have stopped.

[11]Length of famine indicated twice in the New Testament: Luke 4:25; James 5:17.

24

[12]Obadiah tells Elijah of this search, 1 Kings 18:10. Ahab would have started it as soon as he became aware that Elijah's word was becoming true and that no other means would avail to offset it, as, for instance, the Baal prophets.

[13]The later contest on Mount Carmel was really a climax to this one which had continued by that time for three and a half years.

Chapter Three

ELIJAH AT CHERITH

Two questions would have puzzled Elijah as he quickly left the palace area: first, where should he seek a place to hide from Ahab, who would soon be looking for him; and, second, how would he, himself, find food and drink in such a place with this famine coming on? Places to hide would not be such a problem, but where he could also get necessary provisions would. To be near a public market would be to risk disclosure, and to grow his own food would be impossible when no rain would fall.

Consequently, it was a relieved Elijah who heard again the voice of God as he walked along, perhaps not far from the city: "Get thee hence, and turn thee eastward, and hide thyself by the brook Cherith, that is before the Jordan. And it shall be, that thou shalt drink of the brook; and I have commanded the ravens to feed thee there" (1 Kings 17:2-4).

Both questions were answered. Seclusion was to be found at the Brook Cherith, and God would give food by means of ravens, with water being available from the brook. God did not need Elijah to remind Him of his need. God knew better than His servant; and long before. The plan had been complete from the beginning; God was simply revealing it a step at a time. Elijah might have objected even before taking the message to Ahab, wanting to know first how he would fare himself. But he did not, apparently believing that God would, in His own time, reveal the information in just such a fashion as this. An important lesson is seen in this. We want to know all the steps in God's plan before we take the first one. But God wants us to trust Him. He wants us to take a step at a time, as and when He reveals it. The words of verse five are further laudation for Elijah: "So he went and did according unto the word of Jehovah." He directly obeyed. He did not argue first or make suggestive changes, as we do so often. Neither did he complain that his lot would be lonely in such a place. He did not try to improve on God's orders, but took them as given. This is the kind of obedience God desires. He does not make His will known for us to evaluate it. He wants us to obey it, and exactly as revealed.

Cherith

It is believed that Cherith was one of several streams which thread their way down into the Jordan valley. They are much alike, falling quickly from the highland region on either side and cutting sharply chiseled gorges en route. Of Wadi Kelt, for instance, one of these streams and one with which Cherith has been identified by some, W. M. Thompson writes:

> It is a narrow, profound gorge, overhung by tremendous cliffs, absolutely impassable, in whose numerous recesses and dark caverns the prophet could have been most effectively concealed.[1]

Wadi Kelt, however, flows from the west and is rather far south toward the Dead Sea. Many believe that a stream not so far from Elijah's starting point at Jezreel and one flowing from the Gilead region on the east, farther from the population centers and better known to Elijah, would have been more likely.

Walking from Jezreel "eastward," as directed, Elijah would have reached the Jordan in about fifteen miles. Perhaps another fifteen southward would have brought him to the intersecting Cherith. Again turning east, he would have reached the sharply rising ridge lining the valley in about five miles.[2] Here a steep climb would have brought him high above the Jordan where he would have been hemmed in by craggy walls on either side. Small caves in these walls would have greeted him as he stepped along the twisting stream bed, one of which he probably selected as his new home.

Making the cave suitable would not have taken long, and Elijah would have soon been sitting in front, watching the running brook at his feet. Bits of vegetation could have been seen spotting the steep walls, with bushes and small trees occasionally asserting themselves. Straight above would hang the blue sky, cloudless as a reminder of his own prediction. And in the western distance would appear the winding Jordan, visible through the cut of the stream. No path or evidence of human visitation being apparent, Elijah may have noted that God had certainly selected a fine place for him to hide.

The Ravens

When would the ravens come? What food would they bring? How would this delivery work? These questions would have played through Elijah's mind during his long walk, and especially as he now felt the pangs of hunger come upon him. We note the answers he was to learn.

As to the "when," it is stated that the ravens came "in the morning" and "in the evening" (v. 6). Elijah first saw them on the evening of the same day. As to the "what," they brought "bread" (*lechem*, meaning either "bread" or "food" in general) and "flesh" (*basar*, meaning "meat"). Probably *lechem* should be taken in the more general sense. This means his menu was meat and various types of food. The normal diet of the raven is sufficiently varied to fit this description. Writes Gene Stratton-Porter of the raven:

> It is partially a carrion feeder, if offal or bodies are fresh; it also eats the young of other birds and very small animals

and seeds, berries and fruit, having as varied a diet as any bird.[3]

Doubtless in this fact lies a principal reason for God's choice of the raven. Its own natural selection of food would provide an adequate diet for the prophet.

The question of "how" the delivery worked requires more discussion. Some scholars believe that it was purely a natural operation, with the parent birds simply bringing food to their young and Elijah eating what was dropped or left over. The following arguments are given in support: (1) God normally uses natural means when available and they were here; (2) raven nests certainly were present in this gorge; and (3) Elijah would have needed the exercise involved in searching for the food.

Others believe the ravens brought food supernaturally, especially for the prophet. This position is sustained by stronger arguments than the first, and must be accepted. One reason is that the text definitely says that God "commanded" the ravens to feed Elijah (v. 4). This suggests supernatural intervention, not merely a continuation of normal procedures. Another is that the feeding was regular, each morning and each evening. Birds do not naturally keep to this kind of schedule.[4] A third is that Elijah could have found difficulty in procuring sufficient and edible food if he had been forced to search for it. Not very much would have been dropped or left over; and certainly its condition, if found, would have been far from appetizing. One finds it difficult to think that a prophet of Jehovah would have had to take leftovers from birds. A fourth is that this "natural" feeding would not have lasted long enough for the time Elijah had to remain at Cherith. Young birds grow and leave the nest in a few weeks, but Elijah may have stayed there for nearly one year.[5]

It is true that God does use natural means to accomplish His purposes when they are adequate, but here they were not. It is true that this gorge likely did house many raven nests, but this would only have made ravens nicely available for this special service. And it is true that Elijah needed exercise, but he did not have to obtain it by searching for food. This delivery clearly was supernatural, a special "airlift" for Elijah alone.

The first appearance of the birds must have been a thrilling experience. It would have been at the close of that first day, perhaps not long after he had completed housekeeping arrangements. He would not yet have known just how the delivery would be made and so would have often glanced skyward. Then he would have seen them, first high above, and then coming lower into the gorge, and at last settling at his feet—black fellows, sizable, good messengers for the purpose. Soon, with a whir of wings, they would have been gone, leaving behind the precious deposit of food. Yes, how thrilling indeed! God had promised, and here was the fulfillment—his supper, direct from Heaven. We may visualize him quickly bowing in prayer, thanking his Heavenly Father for this wonderful provision. It would not have been a perfunctory prayer—not for this meal, coming like this so directly from God. The prayer would have flowed deeply from his heart, an expression of true gratitude.

We should always pray this way. Every meal we eat is just as much from God; not so spectacularly, of course, but still from God. He provides normally by natural means—a job, wages, a well-stocked store. But all this could be taken away so quickly if He chose. We are not self-sufficient, but always dependent. He wants us to thank Him accordingly.

Lessons To Learn

Often God has more than one purpose in mind when He gives directions to His servants. He desires to provide for their needs, as here with Elijah, but the specific character of those directions may be dictated by His desire to teach lessons as well. God protected Moses in the Sinai wilderness, but it was also a situation where He could teach him necessary lessons in view of the coming leadership over Israel.[6] David wished to be at the battlefront with his brothers rather than tending sheep, but God knew that his encounter with the lion and bear would further equip him for the Goliath meeting.[7] God knows how best to equip His servants. Here with Elijah, at least four factors involved with his stay at Cherith would have presented lessons he could scarcely have missed.

1. Waiting Before God

The first is the lesson of being able to wait before God. Waiting is never easy. One quickly becomes impatient as action is desired. Elijah had to learn to wait at Cherith; and he was so much a man of action otherwise. He had just come from speaking with none other than the king. With challenging boldness he had presented his message. Later he was to defy no less than four hundred and fifty Baal prophets on Mount Carmel, and this with similar poise, even mocking at the noon hour. In these exciting situations he was much at home.

But it was different here in the gorge. At first he could have investigated his new surroundings—the turns, caves, vegetation. However, he soon would have known it all. What would there have been then to fill his long, empty hours? The cliffs, so entrancing at first, would have come to seem like prison walls, his secluded cave a symbol of the lonesomeness he felt so sorely in his heart. Yet he could not go outside for someone might see him. He could only wait, hoping that somehow God would effect the needed repentance in Israel as quickly as possible.

Every Christian needs to learn the lesson of waiting before God. It is easy to think that God's time schedule is incorrect. Paul experienced tedious waiting when imprisoned for two years at the whim of the ruler, Felix.[8] He could have recalled that God had set the Apostles free in Jerusalem (Acts 5:17-21); also Peter alone a little later (Acts 12:5-11); and even himself along with Silas in Philippi (Acts 16:23-26). In this experience, however, God did not intervene. He permitted an unjust Roman official to retain him without cause, and this when there was so much to do. Paul could only wait, believing that somehow God's timetable was right, though it was difficult to see how.[9]

2. Alone Before God

The second lesson concerns how to be alone victoriously. This is not easy either. Man needs friends and companionship. He needs to share his thoughts. He needs to be drawn out of his self-centered world and to recognize that of others. Man's mind is wonderfully made, but it can become his worst enemy when warped with self-pity and evil imagination. Man cannot help but think, and where there are no outside interests he thinks only of himself.

In this light, Elijah could hardly have escaped two problem areas resulting from his being alone. One was the temptation to complain. Complaint is one of the first evidences of a self-centered mind, believing that it is not receiving proper due. A principal item so tempting Elijah before long would have been that which at first had seemed so wonderful—his food. To see the ravens come for the first few times would have been a memorable experience. But the novelty would soon have worn off, and Elijah would have found himself picking over the semi-daily deposit, looking for some variation in the diet! It continued almost identically the same, and he would have longed for a little change. Why could not the birds bring something different? Why could not God provide some supplemental means and permit him some variation? One gets very tired of having the same food every meal.

Then the food would not have been in the best condition. It was carried in the beaks and talons of the birds, which would have tended to tear it. Further, Elijah never knew where it had been found and what the conditions were. Each time he would have had to wash it carefully before eating. Probably the most irritating of all would have been his sense of dependence on the ravens to make the selection of food. God doubtless superintended the birds in this selection, which Elijah must have realized in some degree, but still the psychological factor of dependence on what these birds delivered would have been very real. People like to be independent, and particularly in what they eat. They like to choose their own food. But Elijah had to take what birds brought him. This would have been very humiliating.

This might have been enough to prompt Elijah to complain before long. The temptation could have been very strong. How much he succumbed we do not know, but if it had been extensive, he would have become most unhappy. A complaining spirit is a defeated, downcast spirit. No indication is given that he came to this condition, and so he must have successfully checked the temptation in major part. This would have taken a vigorous act of will, drawing on God for strength; which is to say that he was a good student in learning the lesson God had in mind.

The other problem area is the temptation to doubt. This temptation rivals complaint as a weakness of the mind. How easily man doubts![10] A principal object of doubt for Elijah would have been the famine situation. Was there really a famine in the land? Was he possibly undergoing this deprivation for nothing? Maybe rain had fallen across the Jordan and Ahab was not looking for him at all. Such thoughts would have come only in a moment of weakness, but then like a piercing rapier. Elijah would have responded quickly and strongly: indeed, it had not rained; God had given His word. The doubt would have struck again in another moment of weakness, and then again. Each time Elijah would have had to answer similarly. And so a series of unhappy exchanges could have ensued between faith and doubt. Again, it would have taken a strong act of will, trusting God, to be victorious. Yet, apparently, Elijah was once more a good student.

A meaningful verse in the battle with complaint and doubt is Isaiah 26:3: "Thou wilt keep him in perfect peace, whose mind is stayed on thee; because he trusteth in thee." The state of peace, where complaint and doubt have no part, is attained by fixing one's mind on God. The reason is clear. Complaint and doubt arise when one fixes his mind on himself, as we have seen. Even human association helps. One gets his interest fixed on someone else. However, the highest interest is found in God. With attention centered in Him, one's desires become identified with His. One cannot then complain about what God has provided, nor doubt what God has said. Elijah could not have complained about food with his mind stayed on the One Who had given it; he could not have doubted as to the famine when God was the One Who had predicted it.

This lesson, too, is of paramount importance for the Christian. Sooner or later we find ourselves in this condition of being alone, especially in later life. That time can be one of victory or one of defeat. The answer lies in fixing the mind on God and away from self. It would seem that Elijah learned this lesson at Cherith, and we do well to do the same.

3. *Trusting God for Daily Provisions*

The third lesson concerns trusting God for daily provisions. It involved Elijah's daily food supply. In that the birds came every morning and evening, they brought only enough for half a day's nourishment. This means that every meal presented a new exercise of faith for Elijah. He had to trust that the ravens would come the next time also.

In this situation it would have been natural for Elijah to seek a way of supplementation. The birds might fail sometime. This could have provided some variation in diet, too. But nothing was available. He could not hunt the coney in the rocks, for the animal was unclean. There was no fish in the stream, for the ascent was too steep from the Jordan.[11] Neither could he plant and raise food, for his possible "garden" was solid rock and, further, there was no rain.

He was shut up to God's provision. He could not supply himself. He had to trust that each time the birds would come. This was trusting for daily—even semi-daily—provisions. The Israelites in the wilderness had been taught the same lesson. Manna was supplied daily, and every morning it had to be gathered anew, for all left over spoiled. In this connection, the words in the prayer Jesus gave to the disciples are so significant: "Give us this day our daily bread."[12] God desires all His children to trust in this way. And this is not easy. One tends to look to natural sources, but these are only means in God's hand to make the provisions. He can bring them to nought so quickly. We should praise God for His daily supply by "normal" means just as Elijah did when fed by the ravens.

4. *Trusting When Daily Provisions Fail*

The fourth lesson concerns trusting God when provisions fail. It is one thing to trust so long as provisions keep coming, but it is another to trust when they cease.

Elijah's provision of water finally failed. Water had been the least of his worries for most of the time. Then one day he noticed that the stream was decreasing in depth. At first this would have been reassuring, for this showed conclusively that it had not rained. As the level fell seriously, concern would have arisen. When would new orders come from God? Why did not God tell him where he was to go now? But new orders did not come for some time. Verse seven says that the "brook dried up." The Hebrew word used, *yabhash*, means exactly that. There finally ceased to be any water in the stream. This means that Elijah became very thirsty. He probably even put himself on small rations in the last days, hoping each of those days that God would speak. We note to Elijah's great credit again that he did not take matters into his own hands and move without orders. He might have, as if God had forgotten him, but he did not. He waited, apparently ready to die before moving on his own.[13] He trusted God to bring the further word when the time was right. This was trusting when provision fails, perhaps the highest form of faith. This is challenge for any day. Can we trust God when our job fails and the money runs out? Can we believe that He will still supply when all natural resources seem exhausted? This is a supreme act of faith. Elijah displayed it here. He learned this lesson also.

Footnotes to Chapter Three:

[1]*The Land and the Book* (Hartford: S. S. Scranton Co., 1907), I, p. 398.

[2]The Jordan valley is about fourteen miles wide near the Dead Sea, and tapers narrower as one goes north. The Jordan River winds down the middle.

[3]"Raven," *ISBE*, IV, p. 2533.

[4]It will not do either to explain by saying Elijah went to look morning and evening, for he would have had to go whenever the time was best for finding food, and, moreover, the text says, "The *ravens brought* him bread and flesh in the morning," etc. (italics mine).

[5]Cf. reasons for this, *infra*, p. 61.

[6]For instance, he had been impulsive and self-sufficient when he had attempted to bring deliverance prior to the Midian flight, but his attitude was greatly changed after he returned.

[7]It is likely that both the lion and the bear were encountered during the brief forty-day return to the sheep (1 Sam. 17:15, 16), for he had been at the court for some years prior to this. This would account too for his mentioning the incidents so readily to Saul at the battlefront directly following (1 Sam. 17:34-37).

[8]Marcus Antonius Felix was appointed procurator of Judea about

A.D. 52. According to Acts 24:26, 27, he hoped for a bribe from Paul, and desired to please the Jews.

[9]A pertinent verse here is Isaiah 40:31: "But they that wait for Jehovah shall renew their strength. . . ." The meaning is to wait for Jehovah's own time for action, exactly the picture with Elijah. This involves trust that God's time is best.

[10]Satan worked with this same temptation with Eve in Eden: "Hath God said?" (Gen. 3:1). He engendered doubt first in the fact of what God had said and then in the integrity of God desiring the best for Adam and Eve.

[11]With all such streams drying up annually during the dry season, fish could not live in them apart from swimming from the Jordan.

[12]Matthew 6:11. The word "daily" signifies, basically, "needful" bread.

[13]Job's words here come to mind, "Though he slay me, yet will I trust in him" (Job 13:15). The exact meaning of the last part of this verse is not clear in the Hebrew, but the general meaning of still hoping and relying on God is definite.

Chapter Four

ELIJAH GOES TO ZAREPHATH

God knew the need of Elijah. No one in all Israel concerned Him more. It was necessary to wait with the new orders until the Cherith lessons had been learned, but finally the time came to break silence. We read, "And the word of Jehovah came unto him, saying, Arise, get thee to Zarephath, which belongeth to Sidon, and dwell there: behold, I have commanded a widow there to sustain thee" (1 Kings 17:8, 9). Two parts are found in these orders: an indication of where to go, Zarephath; and an identification of his hostess, a widow.

Zarephath, called Sarepta in the New Testament (Luke 4:26, KJV), and likely corresponding to modern Sarefend, was located on the Mediterranean coast, between Tyre and Sidon, eight miles south of the latter. Sidon was then capital of the region, so that Zarephath, as stated, belonged to it.

Elijah's main reaction was certainly one of joy. He had waited long for these directions. Upon reflection, however, he may have wondered at the wisdom shown in them, for they seemed to counter directly the idea of seclusion. He was now to go to a city where many people would see him, one within eight miles of Jezebel's hometown.[1] It would also be a long walk to get there through other population centers. What was the reason for this change from hiding in a river gorge? Then, also, why ask a widow to care for him? Famine

38

was hard enough on families with husbands. Widows found survival almost impossible. Why burden further one of these?

Puzzled though Elijah may have been, again he obeyed God's instruction without voicing any objection. We read, "So he arose and went to Zarephath . . ." (v. 10). How fine if all God's children were as ready to obey! God desires obedience without excuses and suggested changes.

Elijah's path would have taken him north, up the course of the Jordan, likely skirting the cities near the Sea of Galilee, on beyond the Waters of Merom,[2] and then west over a Lebanon pass to the coast near Zarephath. The distance is about one hundred miles.[3] Walking mostly at night to avoid people, he would have needed four days. Water would always have been at hand from the Jordan, but food would have been a problem. Perhaps God continued the raven supply. Somehow the need was met, and Elijah arrived at the gate of the city.

Why Zarephath and the Widow?

Before following Elijah inside the city, the question of why God sent Elijah to Zarephath and the widow calls for an answer. Elijah probably wondered about the matter all the while he walked. Let us consider the answer implied in the words of Jesus (Luke 4:24-26):

> Verily I say unto you, No prophet is acceptable in his own country. . . . There were many widows in Israel in the days of Elijah . . . and unto none of them was Elijah sent, but only to Zarephath, in the land of Sidon, unto a woman that was a widow.

Here Jesus is speaking of His own rejection by His former neighbors at Nazareth, indicating that He will now go elsewhere since they have refused to receive Him. Blessings which otherwise could have been theirs will now be given to others. Elijah's going to Zarephath is used in illustration. Nazareth's forfeiture of blessing will be like Israel's of long ago.

Elijah was sent to a widow outside Israel since Israel's great sin prohibited this favor to be granted there.

The point to notice is that Elijah was *sent* to the widow. God had her interests in mind as well as Elijah's in giving Elijah these instructions. Elijah was in no way to be a further burden for her, but, on the contrary, to relieve her burden. God wanted to supply her with food at the same time that He supplied the prophet. The good of both was behind the order. An important principle is illustrated in this. Christians should never look for God's purposes solely in what is beneficial to themselves. So often we read Romans 8:28, "all things work together for good," and then equate that "good" with only our own benefit. But God has the interest of all His children in mind. He sees the "good" from the perspective of Heaven in which all His children share.

This does not mean that Elijah's own needs were in any way to be overlooked. God was not to neglect His prophet because of the widow. Zarephath would be a fine place for meeting Elijah's needs also, as the following considerations show. First, Zarephath was outside Israel, and thus not subject to the same careful scrutiny of Ahab's agents in their search. From 1 Kings 18:10 we know that they had been searching, and even in such foreign lands; but this search would have lost its earlier intensity with a year now having elapsed.[4] Second, Zarephath was a coastal town of a maritime country where strangers were common. Elijah's presence would not have called for special notice. Third, Elijah could reside in the widow's extra room on the top of her flat house,[5] and neighbors would have thought only that she was fortunate in having a paying boarder. The term used to designate this room, *'aliyah* (vv. 19, 23), meant such an upper room, usually reached by an outside stairway.

Zarephath would have been as adequate as any place in respect to water and food also. In fact, water does not seem to have been a problem at all, as witnessed by the widow's direct turning to get some when requested by Elijah (v. 10). Probably the proximity of the sea served to keep a high water table in spite of the lack of rain; which means that, on this count, Zarephath was better than an inland city. As to food, the situation was no worse than elsewhere. God had found it necessary to supply supernaturally at Cherith, and would again here, as undoubtedly would have been true anywhere.

Elijah, no doubt, recognized these truths before many days had passed. The new place of residence proved to be altogether adequate in spite of his first questioning. And it was so much more pleasant than Cherith. Here there was something to do, people to see, companionship to enjoy. Days were not nearly so long, nor the waiting so tedious. God was good; His way was best; His wisdom far surpassed Elijah's.

Forfeiture of Blessing

There is also another significant factor in the Luke 4:24-26 passage. It has been mentioned already but not discussed. It is that Israel forfeited for her widows the blessing that God gave, instead, to the Zarephath widow. The implication is clear that God would have turned to an Israelite widow first if it had been possible, just as Jesus had gone to Nazareth first. Jesus had desired to make Nazareth, His old hometown, the center of His Galilean ministry, but the people had refused Him. As a result, He bestowed that honor on Capernaum, where scores of people were healed (Luke 4:31-41). The benefit which the Zarephath widow was to receive would also be great, which might similarly have gone to one of Israel if it had not been forfeited.

Another important principle is here to be seen. Blessing can be forfeited. God will bless those who live for Him and do His will. When disobedience enters, however, He will not bless but grants what might have been to others. It is extremely important to live in the place of blessing. God desires to bless His own, but will not when they live in sin.

In this light, a question arises as to why God chose the Zarephath widow to receive what Israel's widows forfeited. What drew His attention to her? In what way did she qualify when these others did not? Second Chronicles 16:9 delineates those who can expect such blessing as "them whose heart is perfect toward him."[6] Did the Zarephath widow qualify in this way? Had she come to trust in Jehovah? Did Jehovah consider her to have a perfect heart? One finds this difficult to believe for she lived in heathen Phoenicia, Jezebel's old country, where she certainly had been reared in the same religion that Jezebel had now brought to Israel, and for which Israel's widows had forfeited. Difficult to believe or not, this seems to be exactly what had happened, as several considerations witness.

One is found in verse 12 where the widow uses the words, "As Jehovah thy God liveth. . . ." This shows that she knew the name "Jehovah" well enough to associate it readily with one who evidently gave the appearance of a Hebrew prophet.[7] She also knew and used Israel's significant form of oath which asserts that Jehovah "liveth." To employ it would have been quite irregular if she had been a Baal follower, wanting then to give such recognition to Baal and not the foreign Jehovah.[8]

A second reason concerns her remarkably controlled reaction to Elijah's requests voiced immediately at their first meeting (vv. 10-16). He asked for water and she started without hesitation to get it. Then he asked for food, and she merely explained that she had none to give. Need it be pointed out that this was a most gracious response on the part of one who had been experiencing famine at its worst? She was here gathering wood to bake her last cake, and that from a mere handful of meal. Neither she nor her son had eaten adequately in weeks; and yet when Elijah asked for food, that which meant life itself, she was able simply to explain that she had none. No cry of complaint was heard, nor torrent of abuse on one who would dare ask such a thing. When Elijah even asked her to give him what she did have, she also did that, indicating a remarkable faith in Jehovah that He could in truth provide for her miraculously as Elijah had promised. Certainly nothing less than a heart transformed by God could have prompted this kind of gracious spirit and noteworthy faith.

A third reason comes from verse 18 where the widow exhibits a consciousness of her own sin. Her son had just died. She cried to Elijah, ". . . Thou art come unto me to bring my sin to remembrance, and to slay my son!" She thought first of her own sin when this blow fell upon her. She concluded she was unworthy and God, through His prophet, was punishing her. Again, it is only a heart yielded to God which would respond in this way. Other hearts issue in complaint and self-pity. Neither will it do to say that she was thinking of sin only in the sense held by Baal worshipers, as a mere infraction of the Baal ritual.[9] She was speaking to Elijah, Jehovah's prophet, who would be quite uninterested in any failure of this kind. The situation requires that she was thinking of sin as Elijah did. She was conscious of having displeased Jehovah, which means that she was seeking to follow Him.

A final reason comes from her reply to Elijah following his restoration of her son to life: "Now I know that thou art a man of God, and that the word of Jehovah in thy mouth is truth" (v. 24). The pertinent matter is that she did not say, "Now I know who the true God is." She said, rather, that she was now fully satisfied that Elijah was Jehovah's true spokesman. To have been interested in knowing this requires that she had already believed in Jehovah.[10]

Trial and Reward

This shows convincingly that the widow was a child of

God. This is what qualified her for God's gracious blessing. But how had this come about? How had she come to believe in Jehovah? The text does not tell us. Of course, she may have been a native Israelite who had brought her faith with her to Zarephath. If so, she must be commended for having maintained it in this heathen atmosphere. However, in view of the religious declension for so long in Israel,[11] and also Jesus' words that Elijah was not sent to any of Israel's widows, this is not likely. It is much more likely that she was a Phoenician. But if so, how had she been converted?

It must have happened while her husband yet lived. She would have had almost no outside contact, so necessary, since. Moreover, he could have been a trader with such a contact. Phoenicia was a maritime country where trading was the principal occupation. Judah, where the godly Jehoshaphat ruled, could have been a regular stop. There he could have heard and taken the information home, where he and his wife together would have changed their religious allegiance. Whatever the details, it had happened, and a new life in following Israel's Jehovah had begun.

A matter much more certain and significant is that, since that conversion, the widow had experienced great trouble and sorrow. First, she had lost her husband. Her helpmeet, who had supplied the family larder and shared her joy at the birth of a little boy, had been taken from her. We are not told how this happened either, but only that she was a widow. It could not have been many years before the story opens, however, for the boy was still young. The wound was yet fresh and she felt the loss keenly.

Then the famine had struck. Being a widow, it had affected her all the more. This, too, caused her to miss her husband. Her son had been a constant source of comfort, but he also added responsibility. Food had been so expensive and wage-earning jobs were almost nonexistent. Her best efforts had not been able to keep the household supplied. Her continually dwindling food and money had pointed ahead to the inevitable day when all would be gone, which day arrived when Elijah came on the scene. This was trouble and reason for sorrow of the greatest proportions. We can easily think of such an one as extremely anxious and discouraged.

In this light, what we have seen above as to her faith in Jehovah becomes even more significant. In spite of these momentous matters, this faith was strong and victorious. It might have been otherwise so easily. In fact, she might have returned to following Baal. In a day when all events were related religiously, she could not have avoided wondering if her troubles were not due to having changed gods. Her neighbors would have urged upon her that this was certainly true. So, could she have made a mistake? Was Baal punishing her? These questions would have come and they would have been real. Nevertheless, what we have seen indicates what her answer had been. She had not been wrong. She would continue to believe in Jehovah. Somehow, He would care for her. She would be faithful.

Similar times of testing, perhaps not so serious but still very real, come to all of God's children. Financial reverses, accidents, illnesses, death—all can bring severe trial. One can be defeated by these times of testing, and so experience great unhappiness for long periods of time following; or one can, as the widow, rise above them and go on to a fuller, richer trust in God than ever before. The widow's faith had grown because of having risen above the trial, and so she was able to respond admirably to Elijah's requests. The same can be true for us.

All of this God knew. He had seen the widow's trouble from the start and knew the depth of her sorrow. He had seen, too, her triumph over it all. It was this for which He now chose to honor her. It was this which called for the particular directions to Elijah. It was this which qualified her for the blessing which the widows of Israel forfeited.

The provision which God had in mind for the widow consisted of more than just food. This was a major part, of course. She needed it desperately, and the famine still had two years to run. But God saw more. She had need for a teacher. Had the food been the only requirement, God might still have wrought for her alone. But she needed someone to instruct her in the religion of Jehovah. She had not had anyone, and she needed help. What is more, she desired this, as revealed by her remark following her son's resurrection.[12] God wished to supply, and this called for a personal messenger. God selected none other than the finest teacher in all the world!

It pays to be faithful to God. It pays to trust Him fully, no matter the trial nor how long the time. Sometimes burdens seem too heavy to bear and God seems not to hear and help. We tend to be impatient. But God does hear and will help in His own time. Often His help comes in ways we do not expect. When it does, however, it is always so much better than the way we would have had it. God had these wonderful provisions in mind for the widow. He knew better than she her need and provided on the very day her supply was completely exhausted! His time schedule was right, even to the day.

Footnotes to Chapter Four:

[1]Jezebel was the daughter of Ethbaal, king of Sidon, and thus reared in this capital city.

[2]Today called Lake Huleh, located about ten miles north of the Sea of Galilee.

[3]By straight line, about seventy-five miles, but Elijah's path would have made it at least a hundred.

[4]Ahab would have been able to maintain interest for continued search in his own country better than outside. The inquiry outside likely had begun within three or four months after the start of the famine. God had kept Elijah in complete seclusion at Cherith during this period and long enough after for the search to have died down.

[5]The room provided for Elisha later by the Shunammite woman is called by the same term (2 Kings 4:8-10). It made for privacy, both for the boarder and the family downstairs.

[6]The context of 2 Chronicles 16:9 concerns Asa who at one time (when the Ethiopians came, 2 Chron. 14:9-15) qualified for blessing (cf. 16:8) and at a later time (when economically blockaded by Baasha, 16:1) did not, in that he relied on his own strategy rather than on God (16:2-7).

[7]Of course, Elijah may have introduced himself, without this having been recorded; but, if not, she concluded to his identity only from appearance.

[8]Cf. treatment of the oath form, *supra*, p. 18.

[9]The concept of sin was held throughout the Canaanite-Mesopotamian world, but always in only the ritualistic sense. One sinned when he did not please the deity properly by adequate or correct ceremony, but not in some moral deficiency. Even the gods were thought to steal, murder, lie, etc.

[10]Certainly the widow had been convinced of Elijah's authenticity before this, particularly in view of the food miracle; but apparently this resurrection impressed her yet more and made her certainty of a still higher degree.

[11]Since the division of the kingdom in 930 B.C., at least sixty-five years prior.

[12]*Supra*, p. 43.

Chapter Five

ELIJAH AT ZAREPHATH

Elijah found the widow at the entrance of the city. She was there gathering a little wood for a fire. A few words of unrecorded greeting may have passed between them, but the principal interchange concerned what we have already noted briefly, Elijah's three requests and the widow's commendable response to each.

The Three Requests

To state them quickly again, the three requests were that the widow bring Elijah some water; that she then bring him some food; and that, though she had so little remaining, she give what she had to him. We must now look at these at greater length.

One matter to notice is that they were understandable from Elijah's point of view. He had traveled far and was both hungry and thirsty. Unless God had continued to provide supernaturally, something we are not told, food had been a problem all four days of travel, and water had been since leaving the Jordan. We should also observe that more was involved than merely fulfillment of Elijah's needs. Elijah would not have voiced them if that were all. He was not that unsympathetic toward one in such straits. Besides this, the whole conversation shows a planned progression, as we shall see presently, quite out of keeping with merely casual requests. Still further, reason exists for believing that God had told him to say these things. He could not have known otherwise as to the food miracle, at least, and since his words regarding it are so much a part to all he said, it follows that God had also told him the rest.

As to why God wanted Elijah to voice these requests, the answer is seen in terms of how they would have affected the widow. They would have come to her as matters tending to provoke, which would have tested her ability to withstand this temptation and show herself as living a victorious life in faith. Further, each would have provided an ascending scale of such tests. This would have demonstrated how victorious she had become. How many steps could she take and still acquit herself satisfactorily? Since this is what would have happened, we may believe it was God's purpose. He wished to test the widow yet further-before extending to her the wonderful provision of never-ending food.

The test represented in the first request would have been much the easiest. Would the widow get Elijah some water? Water would have been a little distance away, perhaps near the center of town. It was evidently available, for she started directly to get it. All that she was really asked this first time was to interrupt her present activity long enough to procure refreshment for a thirsty traveler. This was enough, for no one likes to be interrupted. One always tends to think that his own task is more important than another's, and this would have been so true in respect to the widow here, burdened as she was. Still, this test was much less severe than the next.

The next concerned food, that which had been her chief worry for the past several months. A famine existed. Without rain, crops did not grow. What food there was had been brought in by caravan and was expensive. Without farming, there had been little employment and none for widows. She had been rationing her food for weeks, and now had come to its very last. Both she and her son were already suffering from malnutrition. Yet here was this stranger asking for food! What would be her response to this?

The third request would have been the hardest of the three. This time Elijah asked her to give him what little food she did have. This would have sounded shockingly greedy to anyone. How could a person stoop so low? But Elijah quickly added the promise that, if she did, she would then have food miraculously provided for the duration of the famine. This brought direct challenge to her faith. Could she believe in Jehovah this much? She had the handful of meal now. Could she believe that God would really give her more later in this supernatural manner? It is easy to talk about faith, but it is another matter to live by it when one's life depends on it. She had never seen a miracle either. The demand on her faith would have been enormous.

To alleviate the degree of this demand a little, some have suggested that Elijah was not asking for all her remaining meal. It is true that Elijah did add the words, "And afterward make for thee and for thy son" (1 Kings 17:13). However, there would have been little sense to ask for only half of an amount this small. All of a handful would have been little enough for either the widow or Elijah; a half would have been next to nothing. No, he was asking for all of it and by the "afterward" statement was already implying that the miracle would be worked in her behalf.

In this ascending series of tests the widow's faith was to be severely tested. There had already been hard tests in the prior months, and she had remained faithful in spite of trials and the "advice" of her neighbors. But here was more. Could she pass these also? God wanted her to grow yet further in spiritual maturity by demonstrating that she could be tried in this way and still show herself gracious and full of faith. God desires the same kind of growth in all His children. He wants them to develop in spiritual stature as they display a life of true faith. Peter tells us that faith so tested is more precious than gold that perishes.[1] Trials test and challenge us to move on to a life more pleasing to God.

The Widow's Response

We must look more closely at the widow's commendable response also. She could have reacted so differently than she did. This is true even in respect to the first test regarding water. She could have flatly refused to accommodate a stranger in this fashion, or at least to have told him politely where he could get his own. Yet she did not; she started directly to get it herself.

Regarding the food request, she could so easily have replied with bitter complaint, pouring out her sad story and even heaping abuse on Elijah for asking such a thing. How could he, a man, ask her, a woman and a widow, for food? Why did he not get his own? That she did not do this, but only turned and stated the simple facts to him, indicates emotional control rarely found—control that only the grace of God could bestow. Through her prior trials she had learned to live above daily problems—to analyze and cope with them instead of being crushed. As a result, she was able to meet this new source of provocation, keeping her emotions in check and responding with admirable grace. This is victorious living. We do well to follow her lead.

Elijah's third request presented the greatest challenge. Bitter, abusive words might have poured from her lips. He now knew her grievous plight and still asked that she give him the little food she had left. The text says only that "she went and did according to the saying of Elijah . . ." (1 Kings 17:15). He had promised her a food miracle if she would do what he asked, and she believed his words. She had learned to trust Jehovah this much.

She probably went to the well first to get Elijah's water, for he was in need of it. Then she took her gathered sticks and went to her house to mix and bake the cake. Elijah would have watched her go with the keenest of interest. He could understand her feelings, for he too knew the value of food. Would she be emotionally capable of bringing the cake to him? Some time passed while he waited, probably yet near the gate. Then he saw her come from the house again, and she was carrying something in her hands. As she drew nearer, he could see that it was indeed the cake. Could she actually hand it over now and watch him eat it? Yes, she could and did. It must have been an emotional moment. Tears may have stood in her eyes, and perhaps in his. This was her all, made doubly precious through days of rationing. But here she was giving it to Elijah, Jehovah's prophet, believing the promise given.

Did Elijah eat the cake? Did he really take it, as it were from her mouth, and place it in his own? One thinks of David's reaction after his brave men had endangered their lives in bringing him water from the Bethlehem well. He "poured it out unto Jehovah," saying, ". . . Shall I drink the blood of the men that went in jeopardy of their lives?" (2 Sam. 23:16, 17). However, it is likely in this instance that Elijah did eat the cake. It would have been for her good, impressing the full lesson upon her mind. And she was soon to have more, much more, when she returned to the house.

Then would have come the walk back to the house again, back to the "barrel" and "cruse" left empty and waiting just a few moments before. The question would have been strong in the widow's mind: would these vessels truly have more meal and oil in them now? She knew them so well and had used them so long. How could they possibly play a part in such a miracle as this? But she believed Jehovah. He, through His prophet, had said that they would. The meal and oil had to be there. It must have been a tense moment as she stepped into the house, crossed the kitchen floor, and looked down into those containers. Yes, there it was—the oil and the meal—just as Elijah had promised. Joy flooded her heart as she realized the full significance. Now her famine worries were over; and, even more important, here was proof abundant that she had not misplaced her faith all these months and years.

We may visualize the widow and Elijah falling on their knees beside the wondrous supply. Elijah was involved as much as the widow. He was to eat of the same provision and his heart would have responded in thanksgiving as well. God was good. He knew their need and He supplied it. And God would have been pleased, for He desires His children to thank Him. Too seldom is heartfelt gratitude rendered, when so much is due.

The Miracle Examined

The vessels involved in this miracle were pottery jars. The first, called *kadh*, translated "barrel," was a jar often used to draw or hold water. Rebekah, for instance, used it to draw water for the camels of Abraham's servant (Gen. 24:14).[2] It would have been of good size for holding flour. The other, called *tsapahath*, translated "cruse," was a wide-type jar with a handle. It was this jar that David, for instance, took from Saul while he slept (1 Sam. 26:11-16).[3] It would have been smaller than the flour jar and more of a jug or wide pitcher for pouring the widow's oil.

What was the nature of the miracle performed in them? Was it, for instance, a large multiplication of food, as when Elisha supplied oil miraculously for another widow that she might pay her debts (2 Kings 4:1-7)? At that time, a large amount of oil was provided so that it might be sold to raise money.

The answer is definite that the miracle was not of this kind. Only two vessels are mentioned, whereas in the instance of Elisha there were many. More important, the verbs to describe the miracle signify that the two simply did not run dry. In the phrase, "the jar of meal wasted not," the verb is *kalah*, meaning "to end" thus the meal did not end. In the phrase, "neither did the cruse of oil fail," the verb is *haser*, meaning "to lack"; and so the oil simply did not lack. God merely kept sufficient ingredients in the containers for the next baking. Whenever the widow went to get more, more was there. They were not kept full, either, but only from never running out.

This manner of the miracle was for good reason. It was necessary that it work this way if Elijah's presence was to remain unnoticed. Borrowing of jars from neighbors would have invited attention, and so would a pantry full of meal. Such news would soon have spread as far as town officials, and then word would have been taken to Ahab. With the miracle working as it did, there was no reason for people to wonder. They would have thought that the widow's improved economic condition was because she had a paying boarder.

Even so, the widow would have had to discipline herself against loose talk.[4] A little boasting would have been natural. Especially with neighbors having criticized her earlier for having followed this foreign religion, here would have been a tempting opportunity to justify what she had done. Her new Jehovah was doing all this for her now. But Elijah would have warned her against doing so. It would jeopardize God's plan with Israel. One reason for the difficult tests earlier may have been to prove her in reference to this responsibility. Could she put God's interests ahead of her own?

Another significance for the manner of the miracle is that it provided a further and continuing lesson in faith for the widow. It caused her, as Elijah earlier at Cherith, to trust God for daily needs. She had to trust for further supply every time she baked. There was a renewed exercise of faith, which is the way faith grows. Had the miracle worked by a one-

54

time, large provision, there would not have been this constant exercise; and, further, the temptation would have been present to trust in the provision rather than the Provider. God wanted her faith in Himself, even as He does all His children.

Death of the Boy

The widow's home was a happy place following this memorable day. Food was no longer a problem. She was daily reassured in her faith in Jehovah and Elijah was present to give needed instruction. Her little boy was regaining his former health and strength. But one day this changed—the precious boy died. How long a time had elapsed we are not told. The text says only, "After these things" (v. 17), meaning after the first day's happenings. The shock for the mother would have been terrible. It would have been easier when she had somewhat expected it earlier, but now all had seemed so different and good.

Although the age of the child is not stated, he could not have been very old. He plays no part in the story, such as helping to gather wood or entering into any conversation. Also, the mother could carry him, and Elijah took his body into his own arms to carry it upstairs (v. 19). Perhaps an age of four to six is likely.

Neither is the sickness identified. The Hebrew word used, *halah*, is only general. However, in that the text says "there was no breath left in him" (v. 17), the difficulty may have been respiratory. Indeed, since the actual word "death" is not used, some have suggested that the boy did not really die, but was only choking severely. Support is found from the fact that Elijah later stretched himself on the body (v. 21), as if applying artificial respiration mouth to mouth.

However, it is clear that the boy did die. For one thing, the text says that "no breath" remained in him (v. 17). Also, Elijah later prayed, "Let this child's *soul* come into him again" (v. 21, italics mine), and did not merely ask for a return of breath. Still further, Elijah was in no hurry to stretch himself on the body, even taking it upstairs first. Haste, of course, is vital in applying artificial respiration.[5]

The mother's commendable reaction has already been observed, as she said: "What have I to do with thee, O thou man of God? thou art come unto me to bring my sin to remembrance, and to slay my son!" (v. 18). She did not complain or charge God with injustice. She did not show bitterness. Neither did she even ask, "Why?" Rather, she found the blame within herself. She knew she was a sinner and deserved punishment. Oh, how seldom is this kind of reaction found, even among God's own children! The tendency is toward self-justification and then to blame someone else, even God. God is often charged with being unfair. But God is never unfair, nor is He unkind. He knows best, and His will is always just. Where there is blame, it lies with us.

Resurrection of the Boy

Elijah's immediate reaction was to take the boy up to his own room on the roof to pray (v. 19). We may well ask why he did this. Could he not have prayed downstairs just as well, where the mother could have watched? The answer is found in Elijah's own personal sense of the conditions in which he could pray the most effectively. He wanted to be alone, undistracted even by the mother. God, of course, could have raised the boy any place. The difference lay within Elijah himself, his own readiness to pray. He recognized that he must ask for a great miracle. The most fervent prayer was in order, with complete concentration of mind and heartfelt faith. This would be true most if he were alone, undisturbed, unwatched, face to face with God.

Nothing in the life of the Christian can take the place of personal devotion before God. There is a place for public prayer, but it can never be a substitute for personal, closet prayer. Jesus said, ". . . When thou prayest, enter into thine inner chamber, and having shut thy door, pray . . ." (Matt. 6:6). Like Elijah, one can then pray more fervently and effectively.[6]

Elijah's first words in prayer were, "O Jehovah my God, hast thou also brought evil upon the widow with whom I sojourn, by slaying her son?" (v. 20). Elijah was puzzled. Why had God permitted this added suffering for the widow, who, after all, was being hospitable toward himself as Jehovah's servant? It was understandable, after her earlier trials, that she should now be blessed with the daily food, but it was not that this tragedy should be brought upon her.

The answer to Elijah's question can only be the same as observed relative to the widow's earlier tests. This was one more in a series of faith-steps. She had passed the three given the first day in excellent fashion. But here was another one, yet more difficult. God was leading her on to a very high plane of faith, a plane achieved by very few. It was not at all that God took pleasure in her suffering; nor that He was now punishing her for sin. Elijah in no way had responded to her suggestion that her own sin was the reason for this. The suffering was only the temporary means. The end was the high spiritual plane. God desired that she be able to live above the most severe trial and still keep her trust in Him.

A word of counsel is brought to mind here. One should be careful not to point an accusing finger at another experiencing pain. God may only be leading that one on to a similar high plane of faith. Job's three "friends" accused him falsely of great sin. Jesus' disciples were ready to accuse the man born blind, or at least his parents, of the same (John 9:2). Jesus replied that his blindness was not the result of sin, but "that the works of God should be made manifest in him" (v. 3). It is always possible that punishment for some sin may be involved,[7] but this is for the person himself to recognize. Others should not judge.[8]

Elijah showed great faith in his request that God raise this boy back to life. Resurrection is commonly thought of as the chiefest of miracles. Perhaps for this reason men deny it more quickly than any other form of miracle. Nevertheless, it was for resurrection that Elijah here asked. Moreover, he had no prior example on which to base this request, for this is the first of the resurrections recorded. It was certainly easier, for instance, for Elisha to ask similarly as to the Shunammite's son (2 Kings 4:32-37), with the example from Elijah having preceded. It was easier for Paul, too, in the raising of Eutychus, who had fallen while Paul preached (Acts 20:9, 10), having the prior examples from Christ as well as these from the Old Testament. But Elijah was first. This was a remarkable display of faith.

Elijah not only prayed, but "he stretched himself upon the child three times" (v. 21). We have seen that this could not have been an application of artificial respiration, for the child was dead. Why did Elijah do it? It was a deliberate action and so there must have been a reason. The answer is that Elijah was observing a principle in God's normal operation. That principle is that God regularly uses natural laws to accomplish His purposes when and to the extent they are available, and only brings supernatural intervention when they are not. When the sea needed to be divided before the fleeing Israelites outside Egypt, the wind could not do very much to accomplish this, but God used it to do what it could (Exod. 14:21). When the enormous number of quail needed to be brought to feed the Israelites a little later, God again employed wind for what part it could do (Num. 11: 31). And thus Elijah's warmth could warm the child's flesh, and his breathing into the boy's mouth, if indeed he did this, could start the rhythm of lung activity. Together this was not much in comparison with the supernatural requirement to impart life, but still it was something and God was pleased to use it.

A parallel thought provides a lesson for us. It is that God expects His children to use their own natural abilities fully before waiting for Him to intervene supernaturally. God has given abilities and He desires them to be employed. It is quite possible to mistake pure laziness for faith. The man who expects God to find him a job without himself looking for it will not get one. The church that expects God to bring growth without the members putting forth good effort will only stand still. God will help us in doing what we can, and desires that we recognize and pray for this assistance. He will do in addition what we cannot do, as we trust Him to this end. He will not substitute special energies for those He has already imparted naturally.

The result of Elijah's action and prayer was that "the soul of the child came into him again, and he revived" (v. 22). The lungs once more began to expand, the heart to beat, the blood to flow, and the cells to produce energy. The little eyes flickered open and looked up into the face of Elijah. Great joy would have flooded the prophet's heart. How real God was! He had answered his prayer!

There would have been joy too in taking this precious life down to the mother again. She also would have been active in prayer. After seeing Elijah leave with the lifeless body, she would have fallen on her knees. All the while she had prayed, her ear would have been tuned to any possible sound above. What was happening? What was Elijah doing? She could not really have thought in terms of resurrection for of such she had never heard. Yet when she heard feet moving again across the roof, and thought she discerned more than two, faintest hopes would have begun to emerge. Then when the two walked through the door, her joy would have known no bounds. She would have hugged the little fellow as she never had before. He was restored to her; as it were, he was twice hers.

In the days that followed, the blessing of this boy in her life would have exceeded anything previous. He had meant much before, of course, but now much more than ever. God had taken him away only to give him back in greater blessing. One thinks of Job. He, too, lost so much, but he was faithful and God blessed him doubly when the trial was passed. God often works this way with His own. Trials are permitted as tests of faith, but when the tests have been passed victoriously, increased blessing results. There is great reward for leading faithful and victorious lives for God.

Footnotes to Chapter Five:

[1]First Peter 1:7. The "strangers scattered" to whom Peter wrote had also been experiencing severe trials.

[2]The jars, twelve in number, from which Elijah later poured water over his sacrifice on Mount Carmel (1 Kings 18:33, 34), were of this same type.

[3]The water that God miraculously supplied for Elijah in the desert (1 Kings 19:6) was contained in this type of jug.

[4]Depending on the age of the little boy, there could have been a problem with him talking to playmates. However, if he was still very young, as is likely (cf. *infra*, p. 55), he would not have realized that a miracle was being performed.

[5]The instance of Elisha has also been compared, as he similarly stretched himself on the Shunammite's son (2 Kings 4:34, 35). However, again much time elapsed. The Shunammite rode several miles to summon Elisha from Mount Carmel and then he had to return again.

[6]It is significant that Elisha, too, prayed alone in his own room when he raised the Shunammite's son (2 Kings 4:32, 33).

[7]Cf. 1 Corinthians 11:29-32.

[8]Cf. Matthew 7:1, 2.

Chapter Six

ELIJAH RETURNS TO ISRAEL

Elijah remained in Zarephath about two years and five months. First Kings 18:1 says that God's word to return to Israel came to him "in the third year," which means sometime after the completion of two years. Since this indication is made directly after the Zarephath events, it follows that this was in the third year of that time. This fits, too, with the New Tesament notice (Luke 4:25; James 5:17) that the total period of famine was about one year longer than this, "three years and six months," for, as already seen, Elijah had been at Cherith approximately one year.[1] It had been necessary that sufficient time be spent there for Ahab to make his search, both at home and in foreign lands, and for the first strong interest to die down. We must also allow a little time after Elijah's return, perhaps a month, for the contest preparations. We should think, then, in terms of approximately twelve months at Cherith, two years and five months at Zarephath, and one month of preparations.

Religious Situation in Israel

Reasons exist to believe that the time was opportune for Elijah's return. One, quite apart from the story, is that God would have wanted it so, for He does all with plan and purpose. He would not have let the famine last forty-two months if He had not been waiting for an anticipated moment. Also, two matters in the story point to this conclusion. One is the ever-increasing effect of the rain contest on the minds of the people and the pronounced impression it would have made after three and a half years. As observed,[2] this had been a main reason for instituting the rainless period. The people should be made to realize that Jehovah was much greater than Baal, whose specialty was supposed to be in rainmaking. As the months passed, this realization would have grown. The people could not have avoided being so impressed. After forty-two months, this impression would have become strong, particularly when the daily necessity of food was so directly involved. This would have provided an advantageous atmosphere for the Mount Carmel contest.

One even wonders why outright revolution did not come before Elijah returned. The answer must be that Jezebel correspondingly increased her ruthless grip on the land. She could not have controlled people's thinking, of course, and it may be that many of the seven thousand later mentioned by God to Elijah[3] turned to Jehovah during these years. She could have controlled outward action through sufficient police supervision, however. She had the determination to carry it through and the perverted willingness to employ whatever measures were necessary. This ironclad control, however, would have prompted yet greater dissatisfaction.

The other matter is that Jezebel took the serious step of slaying prophets of Jehovah just before Elijah returned, which would have stimulated this public disapproval to an unusual pitch. This was an extreme move. She was the foreigner; the prophets the natives. One does not put his hand on native clergy lightly. Few actions spark resentment more quickly. She would never have chanced it apart from an emergency situation, which situation would have been this same rising tide of dissatisfaction. Her Baal prophets were being shown to be less effective than Elijah and, in the minds of the people, less than Jehovah prophets generally. Elijah was not available, but she could do something about the others. So long as they lived, they served as symbols of that for which Elijah stood. In fact, they were probably enhancing the resentment, urging the people to return to the worship of Jehovah at Dan and Bethel.[4] Their elimination would help.

This move, as noted, would have made the resentment for a time still greater. Jezebel, in her careful assessment of the situation, would have recognized this. Still, she evidently believed that the long-term gain was worth the risk. She would have to take greater precautions for a while, but in time the people would gradually forget. However, until some time had passed, the people would not have forgotten, and this is what made Elijah's return here especially opportune.[5] The atmosphere for change would have been the most advantageous possible. This was the situation which God had known would come.

There is comfort in knowing God controls history. Jezebel believed that she was doing the most she could against Jehovah in slaying these prophets, but actually she was playing into His hands. She alone was responsible for the wanton action; but God, in spite of her, was pleased to use it to further His purpose. History is filled with similar occasions when God has turned man's perverted ways to His use. God is always in charge and His side is the winning side. It is good to be His child.

The Return

We may believe that Elijah experienced mixed emotions when the word from Jehovah to return finally came. He had expected it. Certainly many times he had wondered when God would consider the time right. Although he was a man who liked action, he may have come somewhat to dread it. Life was pleasant in Zarephath, and to tangle again with Israel's royal court was not enticing. On the other hand,

63

famine was terrible and it could not end until he did return. Then, too, it would be nice to know how much the famine had accomplished in turning Israelites back to Jehovah. Was Jezebel as strong as ever? Were the Baal prophets as firmly entrenched? Whatever his emotions, his duty was clear. Accordingly, we read, "And Elijah went to show himself unto Ahab" (v. 2).

The text then observes, "And the famine was sore in Samaria (v. 2). Why should this have been recorded? Of course there was a sore famine. It could not have been otherwise when rain had not fallen in over three years. The answer is that Elijah was freshly impressed with the fact, due to it being worse than he had expected, as he once again came into his homeland. Zarephath had also experienced famine, but it was worse in Samaria. So long as he had been away, inner revulsion had kept him from believing it could be. Fields, long unplowed, lay burdened with dust. Wells, once full, gaped broken and empty. People, saving what little strength remained, were seldom seen, and those who were presented bodies like skeletons. The country had suffered terribly. How serious had been the request that Elijah had made three and a half years before! How serious too the sin which had necessitated it! Relief-bringing revival should be effected as soon as possible. Elijah should see the king without delay.

Obadiah

The main item of business as Elijah contemplated meeting Ahab was to arrange a decisive contest with the Baal prophets. The rain contest had been in process for these years, but there was need now to bring a climax. To hold such a contest, the king's permission and assistance were needed. Ahab should be found directly. However, it was not to the king that God first led His prophet. It was rather to a chief officer of the court, named Obadiah, who could act as an intermediary. Before considering the main meeting which did result, some matters of importance respecting this preliminary contact call for notice.

1. *A Compromising Believer*

One matter is that Obadiah as a person presents a sad but true picture of what it means to compromise as a believer, and so provides a lesson of warning. Several verses of the text are devoted to this man, and the principal reason for this much attention is clearly to depict him in this characterization.

We may be sure that he was a believer. We read plainly in verse 3, "Now Obadiah feared Jehovah greatly." His name is also significant, meaning, "servant of Jehovah." Godly parents come to mind. Next, verse 4 tells of his brave rescue of a hundred prophets of Jehovah from the hand of Jezebel, certainly a courageous act by one who must have feared the true God.

Still more reasons exist that he was a compromiser in this belief. One is the very fact that he continued to hold his high position in the royal court.[6] We have seen something of the measures which Jezebel was willing to take in controlling her country for Baal. She would not have permitted any known Jehovah follower to work directly in the palace. Obadiah could only have continued in this position by keeping silent as to his religious allegiance.[7]

Other reasons arise from his manner of conversation with Elijah at this meeting. For one thing, he gave no welcome to Elijah as a fellow believer. He should have been delighted to see him, to compare experiences from the past difficult years, and to report on events at the palace. But none of this was forthcoming. The text says merely that he "knew" Elijah, "fell on his face" in this recognition, and then asked, "Is it thou, my lord Elijah?" (v. 7). Since it is said that he did know Elijah, the closing question must have been only a form, a sort of substitution for the warm welcome that he should have given.

Further, Obadiah even showed resentment toward Elijah. Elijah asked him to tell Ahab, "Behold, Elijah is here" (v. 8). He expected ready acquiescence. Instead, Obadiah immediately objected that to comply might work to his own hurt. The reasons he gave show that he wished he had not met the prophet.

Again, the nature of his fear is significant. He believed that the king might take his life. His reasoning was as follows: the king had put forth great effort to find Elijah and so would take any announcement that he had been located very seriously; hence, if he, Obadiah, should now make that announcement and then Elijah not be found, the king would be angry and take his life. Obadiah believed that the "Spirit of Jehovah" might carry Elijah away so that he would not be discovered. How strange this reasoning in view of the crucial issues of the hour! It shows what the nature of his thinking had been in past days—centered in his own welfare and preservation. He had become accustomed to think first of self-protection as he tried to remain in the good favor of a Baal-worshiping court.

Moreover, he displayed a distrust of Jehovah and His prophet. This is seen in the words just alluded to: ". . . As soon as I am gone from thee . . . the Spirit of Jehovah will carry thee whither I know not . . ." (v. 12). He thought Jehovah might trick him. What a low view of the One in Whom he believed! And how deficient the knowledge! Two matters could have accounted for it: first, lack of interest in knowing the truth, which again fits the picture that his interest was elsewhere; and, second, too much influence of the Baal concept, for Baal was thought capable of such deception.

We should notice too that Obadiah evidenced no concern for his country's welfare. Not once did he mention famine or suffering, or show interest that they be stopped. Elijah, who alone could do something about it, was standing before him. Ahab had even looked extensively for him that he might do so, but all that Obadiah could think of was his own safety before the king. Even a normal humanitarian spirit should have prompted something better, to say nothing of his faith in Jehovah. Obadiah's self-centeredness was very pronounced.

Finally, there was his resort to a defense measure in trying to justify himself before Elijah. Quite uncalled for otherwise, he stated two virtues regarding himself in an attempt to show true belief in Jehovah: first, that from his youth he had feared Jehovah (v. 12); and, second, that he had rescued the hundred prophets of Jehovah (v. 13). The fact that he believed it necessary to cite these matters reveals his recognition of deficiency. He wanted Elijah to think better of him than he was.

These facts testify clearly that Obadiah had been sacrificing his testimony for God in the interest of personal gain. In his greed for position he had minimized his faith, lost interest in the true knowledge of Jehovah, and become so self-centered generally that he could not help but show it to Jehovah's great prophet. He was truly a compromising believer and provides an example in no way to be followed. We must always be on our guard. It is easy to let down spiritual standards for the sake of material gain. The lure of money, pleasure and fame is strong and too many Christians are unwilling to pay the price of true discipleship.

What shall we say, however, in respect to Obadiah's rescue of the hundred Jehovah prophets? If he were this interested in self-preservation, why did he risk an effort of this kind? Three factors may have contributed. One is that he had a guilty conscience that needed to be assuaged. Certainly a believer in Jehovah, raised by godly parents, could not have continued in this life of compromise without experiencing pangs of guilt. Guilt clamors for relief by whatever means available. Another is that he had a growing fear that God might bring reprisal. He would have learned early in life that God punishes the unrighteous. He himself was now in this position. Reprisal from God might come at any time. This is, perhaps, the fear of which verse 3 speaks: "Obadiah feared Jehovah greatly." Then, also, he may have thought he saw a possible advantage for himself in this rescue effort. Revolution was in the air, and Obadiah would have sensed it. If such really broke out, he, as a member of the royal court, could be in a dangerous position. It would help greatly if he could say that he had rescued a hundred prophets of Jehovah. He might even be honored.

2. An Occasion of Rebuke

A second matter of importance was that Obadiah, from this meeting, experienced rebuke for his manner of life. Merely to have met one like Elijah would have served to this end. Elijah had demonstrated little concern for himself in his devoted service to God. When asked to convey a message to the king, he had not resisted even though great risk had been involved. Obadiah knew little of this kind of courage. Conscience-stricken as he was, he could not have avoided experiencing the intended reprimand.

An even more pointed rebuke would have come from Elijah's repetition of the oath, given earlier to Ahab: "As Jehovah of hosts liveth, before whom I stand . . ." (v. 15). The apparent intention was to stress to the fearful Obadiah that God would surely not trick him. It would purposely have accomplished more than this in the mind of the vacillating Obadiah. Particularly the element, "before whom I stand," would have penetrated his conscience like an arrow. He knew that Elijah did indeed stand before Jehovah, and he knew that he did not. He, Obadiah, was a compromiser, lacking courage and fearing for his life. He should be like

Elijah, but he was not. What was more, Elijah's use of this particular oath suggested that he knew this weakness of Obadiah and intended the rebuke he felt. Obadiah's defense statements had not fooled the prophet. If Elijah knew, so did Jehovah. Reprisal might be close at hand. He should change his ways. This thinking would have prompted him to accede to Elijah's request, as we know he did. He went to find Ahab.

3. A Psychological Advantage

A third matter of importance was that Elijah could gain a psychological advantage for his later meeting with Ahab by having Obadiah act as intermediary. Ahab would now have to come to him, and not he to Ahab. The advantage in serious conversation is always with the one who is sought out. The other party is placed in the position of a favor-seeker. Important people call others to see them. Elijah needed Ahab's full cooperation in arranging the contest. This advantage would help to obtain it.

Footnotes to Chapter Six:

[1]A period of twelve months fits this requirement well. However, it could have varied from this as much as two or three months either way. The stay at Zarephath would have varied accordingly.

[2]*Supra*, p. 22.

[3]Cf. 1 Kings 19:18 where God speaks to Elijah on Mount Horeb.

[4]These prophets were not likely true prophets of Jehovah, but like those later in chapter 22, and so advocates of the Dan and Bethel worship. Since Ahab had at that later time four hundred, it is likely that the same number lived at this time. If so, Jezebel succeeded in killing three-fourths of them.

[5]Evidence that the slaughter had not occurred long before Elijah's return is found, not only in that it would have made the return thus opportune, but also that Obadiah was yet successful in hiding the hundred prophets he had rescued. It is not likely that he could have maintained this success very long when Jezebel held this grip on the land.

[6]He is said to have been "over" (*'al*) Ahab's house. This means that he was some sort of superintendent, an important position. Also,

in that Ahab asked him alone to help in locating pasturage for the animals, it is evident that his position was high.

[7]This situation cannot be compared either with that of Joseph at Pharaoh's court or Daniel at Nebuchadnezzar's, as some have done. These two heathen kings had no quarrel with the religion of these men. But Jezebel was engaged in strong competition with Jehovah worship and even recently had taken the lives of the prophets. It is unthinkable that she would have permitted anyone in her employ whom she did not believe altogether loyal to her program.

Chapter Seven

PREPARATION FOR CONTEST

Obadiah's words to Ahab, when he had found him, would have brought joy to the king's heart. He had looked long for Elijah and now he had been found. Perhaps, at last, an end could be brought to the terrible famine. This, however, would have been followed by a new concern. How could he persuade the prophet, now found, to make rain fall again? What price might he demand? It would involve Baal worship, he could be sure, but what might the prophet require in connection with it? If it was its complete elimination, there would be a problem with Jezebel. She would never consent. But the country had to have rain.

Ahab's Question

Ahab's opening question upon meeting Elijah, "Is it thou, thou troubler of Israel?" (1 Kings 18:17) must be viewed in this light. In that he referred to Elijah as "thou troubler of Israel," one might think that the king was angrily accusing the prophet. But he was not, for he was too dependent on his good will. He did not want to embitter him and perhaps make the price yet higher. He was concerned only with doing whatever was necessary to stop the famine, which truth will appear even more as we proceed.

Ahab was interested in Elijah's certain identification. He wanted to know for sure if the man before him was truly the

71

long-sought prophet. There had been contact between them only once and then not for long and without great attention on Ahab's part. Later it had been difficult for Ahab to remember what the strange fellow had looked like. Because the issue was so important, Ahab did not want to be deceived.

However, if Ahab was not thus accusing Elijah, why did he refer to him in this uncomplimentary manner? Why did he not use his name,[1] or call him "that prophet who said it would not rain"? The answer is that this uncomplimentary manner had been the way in which Ahab had been referring to Elijah all during the prior, difficult months, and it just slipped out again without real intention. To Ahab, Elijah had been Israel's troubler. It was with his announcement that the trouble had started. This fact had characterized Elijah in his mind and influenced the habitual way in which Ahab referred to him.

Elijah's Answer

Elijah's answer was fearless and pointed: "I have not troubled Israel; but thou, and thy father's house, in that ye have forsaken the commandments of Jehovah, and thou hast followed the Baalim" (18:18).

He did not answer Ahab's question in so many words, but words were not needed. What was more important was a true prophetic manner, and this Elijah displayed unmistakably. He directly challenged the uncomplimentary reference, with the result that Ahab did not repeat the question again. Evidently he was convinced of the identification. Besides, he was undoubtedly quite taken back with the audacity displayed. Not often did anyone speak to him like this. Although momentary resentment may have flared, he did not show it. This speaks further of his desire to court Elijah's favor.

Elijah's rebuke for Ahab's uncomplimentary reference

was altogether proper even though the king had not used it intentionally. Elijah knew that it revealed the thinking of the king for the past months, but this needed to be corrected. Ahab himself was the real troubler of Israel. He and his queen had caused the people to sin, and this had called for the punishing drought. This must be understood and acknowledged if God was to repent and provide desired relief.

Elijah then went further and identified Baal worship as the particular wrong causing the dry years, saying, ". . . and thou hast followed the Baalim" (v. 18). Elijah had not been this specific forty-one months before at the first meeting. At that time he let Ahab come to this conclusion for himself. It was necessary now to bring this in specific terms. Ahab could not be permitted to rationalize some other cause any longer. God would not otherwise send rain. Also, this recognition was necessary if Ahab was to cooperate in arranging the Mount Carmel contest.

Here again Elijah's great courage stands out. He was talking to no one less than the king, and risking severe punishment; but he knew this rebuke was necessary if relief for the land was to be brought about. It was his task to impart it, and so he did, no matter the peril. What a challenge he provides!

What a challenge this was also to Obadiah, standing nearby watching. Obadiah was not used to hearing people talk to the king this way. He, along with the others, had only catered to the king's favor, seeking benefits, fearing to offend. Here was something different. Here was a real man, not a favor-seeker. Here was selfless courage— knowing the right and doing it. Here was demonstration of what Elijah had implied earlier in his employment of the oath. Obadiah had experienced rebuke then; this would have enhanced it. Elijah not only spoke of standing before Jehovah, he did it. The question comes as to whether Obadiah profited from this example. One likes to think so, and

73

maybe he did. We do not know for he is not mentioned in Scripture again.

Elijah's Directives

Without interruption, Elijah continued with the main order of business as to contest preparation: "Now therefore send, and gather to me all Israel unto Mount Carmel, and the prophets of Baal four hundred and fifty, and the prophets of the Asherah four hundred, that eat at Jezebel's table" (v. 19). The prophet wanted two groups of people to be present on Mount Carmel—the people of Israel and the prophets of the Baal cult.

Who did Elijah mean by "all Israel"? Not everyone, for so many could not have viewed a contest. He wanted representatives from all Israel; and he wanted important ones who could influence others. Little would be accomplished if only a few who lived nearby would come. The object was to prove to all the people that Jehovah was the true God. He wanted Israel's leaders from all cities and areas, and this is the reason why the king's invitation was necessary. Leaders would not have dared to grace an occasion of this kind otherwise. Jezebel could have their jobs shortly, if not their lives. But a royal invitation would make it safe. Besides this, the king had the means for effecting the invitations. He would not have to visit all personally, as would Elijah, but by means of official posts could contact everyone efficiently and quickly.

Elijah mentioned two groups of prophets—four hundred and fifty prophets of Baal and four hundred of Baal's female counterpart, Asherah.[2] Jezebel had a total of eight hundred and fifty prophets to spread and maintain her religion. Elijah asked that all be present, possibly for two reasons. The more he would defeat in the contest, the greater would be the psychological effect on the people. Also, the more present, the more who would die when the contest

74

was over; for, without question, Elijah already anticipated this aspect of the contest day.[3] The more who died, the greater would be the blow to the religion. When the day of the contest did arrive, however, not all eight hundred and fifty were present. Likely Jezebel objected so strongly that Ahab relented on this score. But four hundred and fifty of the Baal prophets did appear, and this still shows real strength on Ahab's part. Jezebel would have objected vigorously to these, and certainly the prophets themselves would not have wanted to come. They were already in control and so had everything to lose and nothing to gain by such an occasion. Certainly Ahab did assert himself.

The place Elijah designated at which these groups were to assemble was Mount Carmel, a prominent ridge jutting out into the Mediterranean just south of the Bay of Acre, running about twelve miles south-southeast into the mainland at an average height of fifteen hundred feet. Why was this mountain selected? It was not really central in the land, nor was it particularly close to either Samaria or Jezreel, the two palace cities.

The answer is suggested by the mention later in the story of a former altar to Jehovah there which now lay broken down (18:30). The altar evidently had been erected many years before, probably by dissenters from the false calf worship,[4] and so stood symbolically for true worship of Jehovah. In its place now stood a grand altar to Baal.[5] As a consequence, this location told in picture form the story of Israel's recent religious history: Jehovah worship broken down and Baal worship entrenched in its place. Thus it provided a fitting background for what Elijah intended to do. As the people watched,[6] he would rebuild Jehovah's broken altar after Baal's new one had proved ineffective; and when the fire fell it would illustrate how God's blessing would again fall all over the land if His worship were similarly restored.

Though the story does not say so, Elijah must have directed Ahab to supply two other items for the contest. One was the water Elijah would need to pour over his sacrifice (18:33-35). He was to use twelve large containers of it, and there was no spring flowing on Mount Carmel after these years of drought. Someone would have had to bring it especially, and the king would have been best able to commandeer such a valuable cargo. The plentiful supply of salt water from the Mediterranean could have been used, but Elijah may not have told Ahab the purpose, desiring an element of surprise in pouring it over the sacrifice. Not knowing, Ahab would have provided good, fresh water, and at considerable cost. The other item was food necessary to satisfy a large gathering of this kind. Visiting dignitaries could not be expected to bring their own. A large amount would have been necessary too, again at great cost in view of the famine.

Did Ahab really understand that Elijah intended to hold a contest? The text does not record Elijah saying this in so many words. However, Ahab did. Everything that Elijah said is not recorded. Ahab had to know in order to do what Elijah asked. He would have had to tell the people whom he invited the nature of the event they were to attend. In addition, the Baal prophets would have wanted to know that to which they were being ordered to come. Surely Jezebel, in her vehement, intervening conversations with Ahab, would have insisted on every detail. Ahab knew and was quite aware of the implications as he turned from the prophet with the directions fresh in his mind.

Ahab's Response

Ahab's response to these directions was quite amazing. We read, "So Ahab sent unto all the children of Israel, and gathered the prophets together unto Mount Carmel" (v. 20). He voiced no objection to being so ordered by a mere prophet. Kings ordinarily take pride in giving orders, not receiving them. And these were orders, not merely requests. Elijah was not simply asking whether the king would be willing to do these things. The verbs employed are imperatives, signifying commands. The king should comply, and he did without voicing objection.

Neither did the king try to change the plans, but carried them out as given. The natural inclination is always to change. This serves to save face for the one commanded. He can thus insert something of himself into the orders and so find them easier to obey. But Ahab did not even do this. He simply proceeded to do what Elijah had told him. He "sent unto all the children of Israel" to invite them, and "gathered the prophets together unto mount Carmel" (v. 20). Food, too, was provided (vv. 41, 42),[7] and water to pour over Elijah's sacrifice (vv. 33-35). How much Jezebel objected to it all, we can only guess. Doubtless many heated words were exchanged, but Ahab held firm. The contest was arranged.

What accounted for this surprising response? The reason is clear: Ahab wanted rain and was willing to do whatever he could to get it. In fact, he may have been somewhat relieved that Elijah did not ask for more; as, for instance, the immediate withdrawal from the land of all Baal prophets. This he could not have effected. But he could make these contest preparations and was quite willing to do so.

It should be noticed too that Elijah did not really make any promise of rain. The subject was not even mentioned. Ahab obeyed without oral or written contract. Of course, he believed that rain had been implied. Its need was too much in the picture to be otherwise. He believed that if he did what Elijah told him, rain would soon fall.

How easily God controls history! Man thinks himself independent and self-contained. Kings and rulers become arrogant and proud. They make the decisions and do not have to listen to others, not even God. Ahab, forty-one months before, never would have believed that he would now be obeying the commands of a mere prophet, and glad to do so. Yet, here he was. God had found it necessary only to withhold rain for these months and suddenly all was changed. The king was no longer independent, making the decisions. He was taking orders from Jehovah's prophet, and hoping that Elijah might be willing to retaliate by granting him the favor of rain.

We may be sure that Ahab felt this humiliation. This was not easy. Every invitation to the people he issued and every order to the Baal prophets he gave came hard. He was not his own boss. Humiliation before God is necessary and good. The authority of God should be recognized by all rulers— not only in times of distress, but always. God blesses the land whose rulers recognize their dependence and ask for His help. God's children have an obligation to pray that this dependence may be acknowledged, and that trust may be shown in God; and that God in turn will grant the rulers the wisdom and ability they need in their divinely appointed tasks.

Footnotes to Chapter Seven:

[1]Of course, Ahab may not have known Elijah's name. There had been no introduction at the first meeting, and there may not have been any opportunity to learn it since.

[2]The goddess, Asherah, is well-known from the Ras Shamra texts, though appearing there as the consort of El. In south Syria, she evidently was considered the consort of Baal, son of El. Her carved pole regularly appeared alongside Baal's altar; Gideon, for instance, being instructed to cut it down in Judges 6:25. Later Josiah commanded ". . . all the vessels that were made for Baal, and for the Asherah . . ." to be destroyed (2 Kings 23:4).

[3]Elijah, with the help of the spectators, did slay the four hundred and fifty who came (18:40).

[4]This altar would hardly have still been there, from pre-Jeroboam days, a period of over seventy years. Moreover, it would not likely have been built at that earlier time, for altars were not permitted indiscriminately in the land, but only wherever Jehovah

recorded "his name" (Exod. 20:24). However, God would have been pleased if dissenters to the calf worship had shown their courage in constructing it, particularly in that they could not attend the Jerusalem temple.

⁵It is not definitely stated that the Baal altar had already been erected here, but it is likely. No mention is made of building activity by the Baal prophets on the day of the contest, while prominent mention is made, as if in contrast, that Elijah did rebuild his. Also it fits the story if Mount Carmel had been made a religious center of Baal worship. This would account for the destruction of the former Jehovah altar and provide another reason for selecting Mount Carmel as the contest location. Further, it would have been easier to persuade Baal prophets to be present when the place was their own worship center.

⁶It is significant, as shall be observed later, that Elijah did wait to rebuild his altar until he had called the people over to him. If there had not been reason for waiting, he would have done this beforehand to save time.

⁷Elijah, on the evening of the contest day, told Ahab to go "up, eat and drink" (18:41) with the people. This means there was a general area of eating, which certainly suggests a provision of this kind.

Chapter Eight

THE CONTEST

Few days have promised greater potential for good than the day Elijah met the prophets of Baal. Forty-two months had been invested in preparation. Now was to be the climax. In one dramatic demonstration, Jehovah would prove Himself the one true God, bringing complete discredit on Baal. Revival should follow. All Israel should again turn to the worship of Jehovah.

The time of the year was spring, late April or early May. Elijah's initial contact with Ahab three and a half years before had been in the fall, at the time when rain otherwise was expected.[1] The place was somewhere on Mount Carmel, and the traditional site, el Morhaka, is as likely as any. The Kishon riverbed, long now devoid of water, could be seen a thousand feet below to the north, and the blue Mediterranean a few miles distant to the west. Enough time had elapsed since seeing Ahab for the king to have made the necessary arrangements, and for Elijah to have felt the pulse of the people for the purpose of planning specific strategy.

Perhaps as many as fifteen hundred spectators were on hand. There were four hundred and fifty prophets of Baal, and when Elijah later ordered that none be allowed to escape (1 Kings 18:40), there were enough people to carry out this directive. This would have required at least three or four times as many people as prophets. They were important persons too, as has been noted. Elijah had wanted key individuals who could influence others. Among them was the king, himself (v. 41).

Elijah's Opening Words

Elijah's first words were a challenge to action: "How long go ye limping between the two sides? if Jehovah be God, follow him; but if Baal, then follow him" (v. 21). Elijah had discovered that the people were divided in opinion. Some did wish to return to Jehovah, having become persuaded when Baal had not been able to make it rain. Others did not, or at least hesitated because they were fearful of Jezebel. They were "limping" as a nation and incapable of healthy progress. They needed to be united, to throw off their fear of the queen, and to decide who was the true God. It has been said that it is better even to decide wrongly than not to decide at all. The person accomplishes little who cannot make up his mind. Elijah knew that if the people would just be willing to decide, Jehovah would shortly show them which way this should be done.

Elijah also wanted the people to notice the uneven odds, saying, "I, even I only, am left a prophet of Jehovah; but Baal's prophets are four hundred and fifty men" (v. 22). It would be well, when the contest had been won, that the people had realized this unevenness. The psychological effect would be greater. Too, this recognition would impress them that the number of adherents never determines truth. The issue was not whether God or Baal had the most followers, but which was the true God. People too often judge on the wrong basis. Popularity is attractive, but truth is the criterion.

Elijah had purpose also in saying that he was the only prophet of Jehovah "left." There had been others, at least in name, but Jezebel's cruelty had vented itself on them. Elijah desired this wanton act to be brought freshly to the people's minds and used this way of doing it. The accompanying resentment would help bring the desired response later in the day, particularly in view of his plan to slay in turn the prophets of Baal.

Then Elijah followed with his instructions. It is noteworthy that the Baal representatives permitted him to give them, for they controlled the religion of the country and were in the majority. We may be sure that this was not a gesture of generosity on their part. The reason must be that they had been ordered to do so by Ahab. They were to do as Elijah directed.

The instructions were simple. Each side should prepare a bullock for sacrifice, with all preparations normal except for the absence of fire. The contest would be whether Jehovah or Baal would ignite the sacrifice supernaturally. The Baal prophets could have their choice of an animal, and would proceed first. With this, Elijah was again seeking psychological advantage. It would show him generous in the eyes of the people and later magnify his victory when it came; the Baal prophets would seemingly have enjoyed an extra benefit, and still lost.

This contest for fire was well-chosen. Both heathen mythology and Israel's own history made supernatural fire to be the highest way that divine approval could be shown for a sacrifice. Heathen priests even tried to deceive by concealing fire under an altar and declaring that it had been sent by the god.[2] Jehovah had already kindled Israel's altars more than once.[3] Elijah's proposal would have found good response in the minds of sympathizers on both sides; it would be a fine way to determine who was the true God.

Two other reasons made this a good test. One concerns what has already been observed regarding the qualification of Mount Carmel for this contest, namely, the presence there of the two contrasting altars, a broken one to Jehovah and a fine, new one to Baal.[4] The fire contest gave use to

82

them in the effective manner desired. The other is that this test would have been decisive and immediate. The result would be made plain that same day. The rain contest had been exactly right for its purpose, but it had taken months to reveal the winner. Now, at this climactic time, an immediate indication was essential.

Baal Prophets' Futility

The Baal prophets readily accepted Elijah's generosity, proceeding first in their selection of an animal and calling "on the name of" their god for fire (v. 26). They seemed to be confident as they began, perhaps due in large part to this being their accustomed place of sacrifice. Though the request was unique, Baal, recognizing the unusual circumstances, should be prevailed upon to answer. However, when fire was not forthcoming, concern began to grow. In time they began to leap "about"[5] the altar, and, following the noon hour, even to "cut themselves after their manner with knives and lances, till the blood gushed out upon them" (v. 28)

This final activity has been called, probably correctly, a display of ecstatic frenzy, a practiced device of the day used normally to receive "revelation" from the deity. It was employed especially through Syria, Asia Minor and Greece.[6] The devotee would seek loss of self-control that his mind might be released for the divine utterance. Rhythmic dancing was often used to gain this release, as were poisonous gases and narcotics.[7] Usually another person stood by to act as interpreter of any sounds uttered. In this instance the loud crying, the leaping and the self-mutilation were all in keeping with this type of activity.

The adaptation was novel, however, for these prophets were not seeking revelation but fire. They were using a device they knew well to seek response in an area they did not. Their mythology told of supernatural fire, but their prescribed ritual undoubtedly made no provision for receiving it. Accordingly, they were proceeding by a sort of trial and error method. If quieter measures did not avail, then use those more violent.

Another feature was also novel. They were involved in a unique contest. The idea of a contest in general was not new. Rivalry among the gods was common to their thinking. But the winner was always decided on the battlefield or in terms of a country's prosperity. Here it was to be determined on an altar, where one either won or lost decisively, and with no way to "explain" possible defeat. The issue, too, was unusually vital. If they should not win, they could expect a great change for Baal worship in Israel, and perhaps lose their jobs. As it turned out, they even lost their lives.

We do well to notice here that great contrast exists between this pagan way of contacting the deity and the way ordained by Jehovah for His prophets. The pagans sought for loss of consciousness, but God says, "The spirits of the prophets are subject to the prophets; for God is not a God of confusion, but of peace" (1 Cor. 14:32, 33). God gives minds to men, with the capacity of self-consciousness and self-control. He expects both to be used. Man was not made a personality that his powers be set aside when God would communicate with him. It is in his personality that man especially reflects God's image, and God desires to speak to and through that image at any time of revelation. A main reason, in fact, for crowning man with that image was that revelation might be possible. Elijah's procedure here later in the day illustrates this contrast exactly. He did not cry loudly, leap about or inflict self-mutilation. He gave only a simple, rational prayer, in full control of his faculties, and the fire fell.

This is an important truth to bear in mind in a day when much urging exists for excessive displays in the name of deeper spirituality. We may be sure that whenever incoherence of thought or emotional abandonment is involved, the idea is wrong. Never is loss of self-control pleasing to God.

The question may be asked whether these Baal prophets really thought their god would answer, or whether this was only a desperation move on their part. The question has merit, for these men had never seen anything like this. Also, they were quite familiar with planned trickery to deceive people as to supernatural acts of deity.[8] Was it possible that such men could really believe Baal might perform this miracle?

We may believe that they did. Their mythology told them that it had occurred in the past, and so it should be possible again. Baal would want to defend his honor. He would not want to lose his hold in Israel and so would surely respond. Then, also, the extent of their efforts is a strong indication of this belief. They would not have tried so long or so hard otherwise. Fire would fall if they entreated strongly enough.

How pathetic is the picture! They believed because they had to, and, surprisingly enough, the mind will conform in large degree to the dictates of one's will. Is this not the picture of all false religions of any day? How much effort is expended, how many sacrifices made, how great suffering endured in faiths that are false; and all this when the glorious truth is available, God wishing it to be known everywhere! He invites all to turn and believe in Him Who indeed is true. It is the great task of Christians to carry this message forth.

Elijah's Mockery

The prophets' earnest activity was interrupted at the noon hour as Elijah called to them, "Cry aloud; for he is a god: either he is musing, or he is gone aside, or he is on a journey, or peradventure he sleepeth and must be awaked" (v. 27). These words did not fall on deaf ears. Pagans believed that their gods could be so occupied. Gods were greater in power

85

than men, but similar in desires and actions. These prophets believed that Baal might in truth be talking, or gone on a trip, or sleeping. So they followed the advice. They cried louder and even began to cut themselves to draw Baal's attention.

What was Elijah's purpose in this? The text says that he "mocked" them. But why? The answer is that he wished to stimulate the interest of the spectators as much as possible in his own turn. He wanted the people to look forward to when he would try. This mockery would give him an air of overconfidence, and cause them to want to see if he could make good on it. As a result, increased effort of the opposition would add by showing further the futility of waiting longer for the Baal prophets. If they were so bankrupt that they would even take advice from the enemy, there certainly was little point in expecting any results. Let another try who might be more successful.

There was merit also in the way Elijah brought this mockery. It made for a clear distinction between Baal and Jehovah. For Baal might be involved in such finite, human actions, but never Jehovah. Baal might be hard to contact in prayer because of talking, being gone or sleeping, but never the supreme, infinite God of Heaven. Many, if not most, of the people would really have known this, and would have been resisting thinking about it during prior months, due to the expediency of following Baal. This reminder was altogether appropriate to make the recognition fresh in this contest hour.

Let us not pass this thought without praising God anew that He is not limited in ways of this kind. He is never so occupied that He cannot, or will not, hear our prayer. His ear is always open, and we may pray at any time. It is never too late at night, nor too early in the morning. He is never too busy or uninterested. He will hear when we call.

Elijah's Preparation

There appears to have been a little distance between the two altars, enough so that Elijah had to call the people to him when it was his turn (v. 30). Undoubtedly the Baal leaders, when they had first built their cult center here, had not wanted it too near the former altar to Jehovah.

Before calling the people, Elijah had some work to do, along with the help of a servant (v. 43). One matter was to prepare the twelve stones, "according to the number of the tribes of the sons of Jacob" (v. 31), with which to rebuild the altar. Being twelve, they symbolized the united kingdom and provided something of a rebuke for the kingdom division since Jeroboam. Most of the stones probably laid nearby and needed little more than to have dirt removed from them. Another task was the preparation of the bullock. The actual cutting into pieces should wait until the people could watch (v. 33), but the slaying could be done ahead of time. Finally, there was need for firewood to be made ready for easy access.

The hour when Elijah finally beckoned the people and began his activity is said to have been the time "of the evening oblation."[9] His first action was to reconstruct the altar (vv. 31, 32). He waited to do this with good reason. He wanted the people to see him actually rebuild it so as to impress them the more with the important symbolism we have already observed. As Jehovah's destroyed altar needed to be rebuilt before fire could fall, so Jehovah's destroyed worship throughout the land needed to be restored before His blessing could again be bestowed. Baal's altar had proved ineffective in bringing fire, just as his worship had proved the same in bringing rain. What was needed was change—do away with the false Baal and return to the true Jehovah. If Elijah had built the altar ahead of time, this symbolism would not have been nearly so apparent. The actual placing of the stones in position as the people watched would have given both time and stimulus for the thoughts to have formed.

A parallel truth is important for any day. God's altars, His worship and His work need to be restored to places they once held. There are many churches today which no longer preach the truth of God. There are many schools which no longer train ministers to preach the Bible as authoritative and infallible. There are multitudes of families which no longer gather around a common family altar. Reconstruction is needed with these too. The old altar needs to be rebuilt. The fire and rain of God's blessing will fall only when, and to the extent, this is done.

Elijah's next action was to dig a trench around the altar. The size of the trench is said to have been "as great as would contain two measures of seed" (v. 32). The meaning of this phrase is not clear. If the trench was only large enough to contain two measures (about two pecks) poured into it, it was very small. Perhaps an area was meant of the size which this much would sow, which would have been very large. Certainly it was large, whatever the exact meaning, for it had to contain the water that would overflow the altar. Also, a greater size would have made a greater impression. Elijah then put "the wood in order" and "cut the bullock in pieces," laying these on the wood (v. 33).

Then he astounded all by commanding that twelve pots of water be poured over the sacrifice. This was a strange way to make fire. Normally one tries to insure that everything is as dry as possible. But Elijah wanted everything wet. Also, he wanted a lot of water. Each pot[10] would have held several gallons, and there were twelve. The altar was not large either. The twelve stones, being of a size a man could handle, would have covered an area less than three by four feet. The first four pots would have soaked it thoroughly without calling for eight more.[11]

A principal reason for Elijah doing this was to disprove

any trickery on his part, for, as observed, sometimes heathen priests concealed fire beneath an offering until the proper moment so as to make the people believe it had come supernaturally. This may have been another reason why he built the altar as they watched: they could see firsthand that only solid ground was under the stones. He did not want the Baal representatives to be able to accuse him of deception later.

Another intention was to impress the people further with his fairness and honesty. There would be benefit in having the people think of him as highly as possible. A third intention was to stress his own confidence in Jehovah. All twelve pots would not have been needed merely to disprove trickery or inspire in the people a respect for his honesty. He wanted the people to know that Jehovah, in contrast to the incapable, false Baal, could ignite an altar no matter what its condition, even if drowned in as much water as this. It showed confidence in Jehovah too in respect to water supply. Elijah knew that the people would be shocked at this seeming recklessness with what was to them more valuable than money. This would remind them that he, as Jehovah's prophet, had shut the water off those forty-two months before, and so alone had the right to be this reckless. He had full confidence that Jehovah controlled the rain, as indeed the fire, and could send it again when His servant called.

Confidence of this kind should be manifested by all of God's children. Elijah displayed it when he brought the mockery at the noon hour and he did so further here. He had complete confidence that God would send the fire, and later the rain, and vindicate His name. We need the same. We need to be bold for our Savior. Too often we hesitate and are fearful. In conversation we speak of things other than Christ and His Word. We let the world talk of what interests them. What we need is Elijah's confidence and boldness. We have the truth of God, the most important message that a man can hear. Let us proclaim it with confidence—fearlessly and without hesitation.

Notice should be taken also as to Elijah's careful planning in respect to the whole occasion. Such planning had appeared in his orders to Ahab a month before, in his well-ordered instructions to the prophets, in his pointed mockery at the noon hour, and in the use of water. In this also he provides a fine example. God's work should never be done slovenly. There is a right way to do things which takes real planning and effort, and we should be satisfied with nothing less. This is not to deny the necessity of faith. God's work must always be done through trust in Him; but He uses means and this includes the finest planning and work. Too often what is only laziness is excused in terms of faith, and this God cannot bless.

The Fire Falls

Elijah's prayer for the fire was brief and carefully worded:

O Jehovah, the God of Abraham, of Isaac, and of Israel, let it be known this day that thou art God in Israel, and that I am thy servant, and that I have done all these things at thy word. Hear me, O Jehovah, hear me, that this people may know that thou, Jehovah, art God, and that thou hast turned their heart back again (vv. 36, 37).

These words take about thirty seconds to speak in the manner which Elijah would have assumed; thirty seconds, in contrast to the seven or eight hours[12] which four hundred and fifty prophets of Baal had used. The marked difference must have stood out in the spectators' minds. It is not the length of prayer that brings response from God; it is the earnestness and faith manifested. Mere repetition of phrases has no bearing. Rather, God looks for a right heart.

This prayer was intended for the people as well as God. In fact, it was more an instruction than a petition. One thinks of Jesus' prayer at the tomb of Lazarus, in which He stated: ". . . I said it, that they may believe that thou didst send me" (John 11:42). Not often should prayer be used to instruct in this way, but occasionally there is need. Here the people needed to be impressed that Jehovah was the God being petitioned, and not Baal. Thus the name "Jehovah" appears three times. The mention of Abraham, Isaac and Israel was to make a historical tie, causing them to remember their true heritage.

There were three requests, but they were also in reference to the people. Elijah did not once mention fire or petition God to send it. He asked first that the people recognize Jehovah as the true God, this being stressed by double mention. Second, that they should be reminded that Elijah was Jehovah's prophet and that "all these things"—meaning especially the rainless years and now this contest—were being carried out at God's direction. And, third, that they should realize Jehovah had "turned their heart back again," by which he meant that all this was being done so that their hearts would be turned back again.

The moment must have been tense as Elijah's words died away, with silence reigning over all two thousand viewers. They had witnessed a direct contrast to the manner of the Baal prophets. There had been no frenzy or even prescribed ritual, but only quiet confidence in a clearly-voiced, understandable prayer. Would this bring the response from Heaven? Every eye was focused to see. And, "Then the fire of Jehovah fell . . ." (v. 38). How it came is not indicated. It may have been as a bolt of lightning; perhaps a quickly descending light; possibly only a sudden roaring fire on the altar. But it came, and no one could mistake it. Elijah's prayer had been answered. Jehovah was the true God, not Baal.

But there was more. As they watched, the people soon saw that the fire was not normal. It "consumed the burnt-offering, and the wood, and the stones, and the dust, and licked up the water that was in the trench" (v. 38). Before the last flame died out, not only the wood and meat had disappeared, but also the altar and the water. All that remained were smoking ashes and an empty ditch. Without doubt Elijah himself was surprised. He had expected the fire, but this was extra. God did something more than he had asked.

What was the reason? What need did God see that Elijah did not? It was more than just to impress the people at the time, for the fact of fire at all was enough for this. The reason was that there might be lasting momento of this occasion. God saw fit that there be evidence of this great miracle in days to follow. He knew that doubts can arise when an important experience is past. Did it really happen? Or was there some mistake and somehow something far less became magnified over what it really was? When doubts start, they are hard to stop. But here was tangible evidence to stop them. Here was a pile of ashes only, which anyone could come and see—no stones, no dirt, just ashes where an altar had stood. A pile of ashes cannot be disturbed without showing. Fire that consumes stones and dirt cannot be kindled by human hand. This was evidence to disprove any doubter or any claim of fraud which Jezebel or anyone else might bring. God saw this as a need and met it.

God's grace and wisdom in providing for His children are wonderful. This fact should never become commonplace to us. We need to remind ourselves often. Here God not only provided what Elijah expected, but He gave far more, seeing a need that Elijah did not. We are reminded of Romans 8:26: ". . . We know not how to pray as we ought; but the Spirit himself maketh intercession for us . . . ." Elijah prayed, but he could not see the full need. The Holy Spirit saw it, made intercession in reference to it, and God the Father met it. Sometimes we wait long for God to answer some prayer; and then, when the answer comes, it is quite different than what we had expected. It is normal to be disappointed at first. But later we see the greater wisdom displayed. God has seen a need we did not, or in a light that we did not, and provided better than we knew. God shows His grace and wisdom in this, and we should praise Him with all our hearts.

Footnotes to Chapter Eight:

[1]*Supra*, p. 20.

[2]Chrysostom in his *Orat. in Eliam I*, p. 765, says, "I speak as an eye-witness. In the altars of the idols, there are beneath the altar channels, and underneath a concealed pit; the deceivers enter these, and blow up a fire from beneath upon the altar, by which many are deceived, and believe that the fire comes from heaven." Keil in his commentary on Kings also cites Ephraem Syrus in evidence, p. 249.

[3]Cf. Leviticus 9:24; Judges 6:21; 13:20; 1 Chronicles 21:26; 2 Chronicles 7:1.

[4]*Supra*, p. 75.

[5]"About" (*'al*) can mean "upon" just as well. They may have actually leaped on and off the altar.

[6]Cf. T. J. Meek, *Hebrew Origins* (New York: Harper & Brothers, 1950), p. 155; or E. O. James, *The Nature and Function of Priesthood* (New York: Barnes & Noble, 1959), pp. 30, 31.

[7]Cf. E. O. James, *ibid.*, p. 40; or T. H. Robinson, *Prophecy and the Prophets* (New York: Chas. Scribner's Sons, 1923), p. 31, for good descriptions.

[8]In the Oriental Institute Museum in Chicago, an image of the Egyptian god, Horus, in the form of a falcon is shown. It has two small holes running from the tail through the body, leading to the head and beak respectively, both of which originally were moveable. These holes are believed to have been for strings by which a clever priest, probably hidden, could make the bird give "yes" or "no" answers to questions of an inquirer by a nod of the head or a movement of the beak.

[9]The "evening sacrifice" time of the Mosaic law was about six o'clock. Reference may be, however, to an evening sacrifice of Baal worship, since Israel had been observing this program for some years, and this may have been earlier. The time could not have been late in the day for the Baal prophets were still to be slain and prayer made for rain, both before dark. Perhaps a time around five o'clock is likely.

[10]These pots were the same type as the widow used for her meal "barrel"; *supra*, p. 53.

[11]Elijah called for these pots by groups of four, not all at once.

The psychological impact would have been greater as the people would have assumed each of the first two times that surely this was all, and then there would have been another group.

[12]Proceedings likely would have gotten under way between nine and ten o'clock that morning. If they concluded at five, this would have made over seven hours.

Chapter Nine

THE RAIN

The people gave the desired response as they saw the fire fall. They cried, "Jehovah, he is God; Jehovah, he is God" (1 Kings 18:39). Further, they "fell on their faces" in an act of submission. This showed not only intellectual recognition but also emotional assent. They had been fully convinced as to Who the true God was. The four hundred and fifty Baal prophets had tried so long and received nothing; but Elijah had uttered only a brief prayer and received so much. The thrilling sight of fifteen hundred Israelite leaders bowing low before Jehovah must have greatly moved the heart of Elijah. After all these years, here was real, tangible change.

Elijah did not pause long in the glow of this much of the victory. There was more to achieve, really the most important part. His voice was clearly heard again: "Take the prophets of Baal; let not one of them escape" (v. 40). He wanted these assenters to prove their new acclaim by helping to take the lives of the Baal prophets.

A bit of reflection reveals that this order was the most crucial of the day. These spectators were men of position. They had dared to come here only because of the court's invitation. They had much to lose should they not stay in line with official policy. They could strongly suspect that the invitation had been Ahab's doing, not Jezebel's. They knew well her feeling toward anything relating to the former Jehovah worship. They knew too that these Baal prophets were her special concern. It was one thing, then, to come to this contest and even voice an oral decision, followed by due submission in worship, that Jehovah had won; but it was another to help in slaying these favorites of the queen. All who did could expect the severest reprisal, which could easily include death. That is, this would be so unless change was effected, Baal worship overthrown and Jezebel shorn of her power.

In other words, Elijah was asking for a full commitment to revival. He was asking that they take this stand against the queen in faith that this decisive change would come. The question before them was whether they were willing to commit themselves this far. If they decided affirmatively, they would have to go all the way. There was no middle ground. Revival had to be effected.

For this reason the next words in the text are the most important of the story: "And they took them; and Elijah brought them down to the brook Kishon, and slew them there" (v. 40). The people did accede to Elijah's words; they made the big decision. Elijah would have planned for it when he had first called the people to him around his altar. He would have made sure that the Baal prophets were given the inside positions, where, as it would seem, they could see better and make sure that no trickery was played; but where too they would be surrounded by their potential guards when the order would be given. When this crucial decision was made, all the people had to do was close ranks. The prisoners were inside and unable to escape. But the decision would have had to be made quickly. These prophets would not wait while they hesitated. What a momentous choice to have to make so quickly! Their lives could depend on it. But they made it. They did close ranks and herded together these prophets, now filled with consternation and fear, down the slopes of Mount Carmel to the Kishon river-bed below.

Life is made up of decisions. Some are small; others are large; and a few determine a person's life for years to come. These last are especially important. Often they are not easy to make. Sometimes real sacrifice is involved, if not danger as on Mount Carmel. But they should always be right decisions. At times they must be made quickly. When they are, the decision really is not the product of a moment, but of a multitude of other decisions made long before. We condition ourselves for each new choice by the way we made earlier ones. The people on Mount Carmel did not really make their decision in that brief moment. It had been made by them during the previous forty-two months of famine. In their hearts a resolve had formed, whether consciously or subconsciously, to return to the worship of Jehovah when the opportunity came, no matter the cost. Character is formed by decisions. Nothing is more important in our lives than making right decisions.

The task of slaying so many persons presented a sizable challenge. Elijah could not have done it alone, not in the time remaining that day. We may believe that the guards came to act as both executioners and disposers of bodies when the riverbed was reached. It may be, in fact, that Elijah was occupied fully in just organizing the operation and seeing that it ran smoothly. Evidently good cooperation was given, for the task was completed. It certainly was not pleasant for any, but this is true of many necessary tasks.

It is well to note that it was necessary. We have observed that it was indispensable as a way to solicit the people's full committal. But other reasons existed also. It was the first possible step in the actual deposition of the Baal religion. To be rid of the prophets would be a substantial beginning in the complete eradication necessary. Also, God could not send rain until the prophets, the symbol of Baal worship,

97

were removed from the land. God had stopped the rain because they had come into the land. It was not fitting to start it again until they were gone. The people should know that rain had fallen only after the false prophets had been killed, and so be assured that Baal had had no part. Further, the people at large needed a special incentive, a spark to ignite their hopes, for joining the revival movement. Nothing would do this better than to learn that even the Baal prophets had been killed at the conclusion of the Mount Carmel events. Thus Elijah would loom as a leader capable of making revolt truly possible. Finally, and perhaps most important, God long before had stated explicitly that all such false prophets should be killed.[1]

Prayer for Rain

Elijah had yet another responsibility before dark. He had to pray for rain. Before considering what the text says regarding this important prayer, we do well to note a significant commentary on it in James 5:16-18:

> . . . The supplication of a righteous man availeth much in its working. Elijah was a man of like passions with us, and he prayed fervently that it might not rain; and it rained not on the earth for three years and six months. And he prayed again; and the heaven gave rain, and the earth brought forth her fruit.

In this passage, two prayers from Elijah are highly honored by selection as examples of effective praying. No record is given of the first, when he prayed that the rain stop, but there is of the second, and that is the one before us. In this light, the prayer takes on added significance. It may be assumed too that the Spirit of God, Who authored both the record and the commentary, would have included in the record those features most important for making the prayer thus exemplary. The description is brief, even omitting the words spoken, and so all that is included must be for good reason.

1. *Humility*

The first matter cited concerns Elijah's posture as he prayed: "He bowed himself down upon the earth, and put his face between his knees" (v. 42). This was the oriental position of complete prostration. The person knelt with his forehead touching the ground and his face looking back toward his knees. It was considered the most humble of all positions, kings often demanding it of their subjects.

Why should a description of Elijah's position receive this stress? Prayer posture is not normally so important. It is well to pray on one's knees when alone or when few are present, for it does speak of humility and this should always be the heart attitude. Sometimes, however, there are good reasons to stand or sit. Posture of itself is never a guarantee of efficacy before God. One can be as proud on his knees as in any other position.

Posture in this instance, however, was important, for it signified that Elijah was humble before God in prayer, even though he had just concluded a day that could easily have made him proud. In this way the Spirit of God is telling us that Elijah still remained humble after all the success the day had brought. All day long Elijah had been the center of attention. Others, important people, had listened to him and obeyed his orders, with everything working out just as planned. Even before this day he had been important. Forty-two months earlier he had prayed, and it had not rained since. Then in recent weeks he had witnessed the king himself carrying out his specific directives, with the result that fifteen hundred dignitaries had assembled along with the four hundred and fifty opposing prophets. These prophets had followed his instructions, and at the noon hour his mockery of them had been exactly right. God had heard his prayer for fire and answered in an even greater degree than expected. Finally, there was the climaxing commitment of the people. Yes, it had been a successful day, with all aspects well-executed.

At its close, Elijah might indeed have been proud, thinking himself to be a valuable servant of God, and not thinking in terms of continued humility. This was not the case, however, and this is what the Spirit of God is saying by describing Elijah's humble position. He could yet come on his face as he prayed, in complete submission before God. He was still recognizing that blessing comes only from above. Any answer would not be due to his own abilities, but only as God would be pleased to grant it.

God desires similar humility in our lives, but this is not an easy requirement to meet. Pride asserts itself so quickly, even in one's prayer life; in fact, perhaps the most insidiously there. It appears both in the manner of prayer and the nature of requests. Particularly in public prayer, there is a temptation to display knowledge and language ability. Always there is a tendency toward self-centeredness in requests. Few there are who truly seek God's interests in the petitions voiced. But God looks for humility. It is a prime requirement if prayer is to be effective.

2. *Faith*

The second matter concerns Elijah's directive to his servant: "Go up now, look toward the sea" (v. 43). The words of the prayer have intervened, and now he tells his helper to go up to a higher point on the mountain and look out over the Mediterranean. Elijah, who had returned to the top of Mount Carmel for this prayer, was probably located near the pile of smoking ashes. God had answered so wonderfully there earlier; thus it was a logical place to pray again. Yet it was not the highest point from which to view the western horizon, the direction where clouds might be expected to

100

appear. The servant could see better a little higher up.

Elijah's reason is clear. He was expecting an answer to his prayer. Because he prayed humbly and sincerely, he expected God to answer. Clouds that would bring the rain should already be rising. This was exercising true faith. Elijah believed implicitly that God would respond this quickly and definitely. How much in contrast this is with what is commonly found! Christians so often ask and then wonder; or worse, go home and all but forget that they asked. We are often more surprised when God does answer than when He does not. It is taken quite as a matter of course if nothing happens. The force of the fact here is that Elijah was expecting an answer.

There is also another indication here of Elijah's great faith. It is found in the preceding verse (v. 41) where Elijah says to King Ahab, "Get thee up, eat and drink; for there is the sound of abundance of rain." He spoke these words prior to climbing back up the mountain. He saw the king, who had likely been present all through the day, off to one side. The king was unhappy and the reason was apparent. He had arranged the contest for the purpose of receiving rain, but as yet none had fallen. The fire demonstration had been interesting, but it had not helped with this need. In fact, it had only scorched more earth, and Ahab had too much of that as it was. Elijah, seeing his distressed appearance, detoured to his side to bring a bit of cheer in view of the prayer he was about to offer. The king could go up and "eat and drink" with the others, and so forget his concern, for "there was a sound of abundance of rain."

On what did Elijah base this bold prediction, indicating even, by the words he used, the extent of the rainfall? He used the word *geshem*, meaning a more heavy rain, rather than *matar*,[2] and this yet qualified by the word *hamon*, meaning abundance.[3] He was promising a very heavy rainfall, the kind needed to bring the change Ahab wanted. It has been suggested that God had told him beforehand. However, this will not do,[4] for then Elijah would not have had to pray for it, and especially not seven times (v. 43); nor would James have cited the prayer as exemplary of effective praying. The answer can only be found in Elijah's great faith. Though he had not yet voiced the prayer, he believed fully that God would answer when he did, and this to the extent of making this promise to the king.

Faith is vital to effective praying. One must truly believe as Elijah if God is to answer. This, too, is difficult. It is easy to doubt—if not in words, then in actions. God desires faith in His promise to hear. This means an attitude of expectancy such as Elijah's, who sent the servant to look for the cloud.

3. *Perseverance*

The third matter is found in Elijah persisting in his request "seven times" (v. 43) until God answered. The exemplary lesson this time is that God's children are to persevere in praying.

After the first directive from Elijah, the servant did go up to look, but found no cloud. He returned this word to Elijah along with, no doubt, a discouraging countenance. Elijah's prayer of the afternoon had received an immediate answer, but nothing was happening this time. However, Elijah did not consider this a final answer from God; he prayed again and sent the servant once more. Again the indication was negative, but still Elijah did not quit. He prayed a third time, and then a fourth, and finally seven times, always sending the servant. He wanted it to rain. It had to rain, for there was an obligation to the king, and he, Elijah, had just promised it to him. Great ill would result for future relations with the king if it did not. We may believe that, each time he prayed, he prayed harder. Greater urgency marked his words and perspiration stood on his brow. How many times he would have continued to ask had God not answered on the seventh, we can only guess. Rain had to fall, and he was ready to continue asking until it came.

The lesson in perseverance illustrated here is similar to Jesus' stress in the parable of the importunate widow (Luke 18:1-8). There He summarized the truth involved in these words, "[Men] ought always to pray, and not to faint." The unjust judge of the parable would not heed the widow's entreaty until after extreme persistence. Finally he did because she persevered. Why does God let His children wait in this fashion? Is He like this unjust judge, not wanting to grant favors unless strongly urged? The answer, of course, is "no." The reason concerns us who wait. Either our request is not at the right time, or else God sees some benefit for us in letting us wait. He may want to prove our sincerity in the request. Do we really want it? Or He may desire to test our faith and so engender spiritual growth. God is more interested in our spiritual profit than granting requests.

What spiritual benefit did God have in mind here for Elijah? It was not to prove his sincerity in the request, for this was apparent from the first. Nor was it to test Elijah's faith, for this too was strong. The answer concerns the matter of pride. In spite of the fine, exemplary humility he showed, Elijah was still a man of "like passions with us,"[5] and had to combat pride. He had been waging a fine battle. He had come on his face in prayer. But God knew that it would be easier to continue to do this in future times if his prayer was not answered immediately this time. It had been necessary in the afternoon to answer directly, for the people were watching, and they must be impressed. But here Elijah was alone and could be dealt with alone. It would be better now for him to wait. Let him become a little anxious and perspire. This would help him to remain humble, causing him to throw himself more completely upon Jehovah.

Rain Falls

The seventh report of the servant, that a cloud "as small as a man's hand" was rising "out of the sea," brought new orders from Elijah: "Go up, say unto Ahab, Make ready thy chariot, and get thee down, that the rain stop thee not" (v. 44). The small cloud was all the indication Elijah needed. Rain would soon fall, and the king should hurry for home. The shallow Kishon riverbed could soon overflow with the amount of water that would fall, and Ahab might have difficulty if he tarried long.[6]

The text suggests[7] that, in spite of this warning, the storm still broke before Ahab could get away. Evidently it rose rapidly. The wind began to blow, the clouds to mount, the lightning to flash, and the thunder to roar. Darkness descended quickly, the hour already being late. Rising storms tend to fascinate, and Ahab, having longed for rain these years, may have felt this doubly. This may be one reason why he did not leave sooner. He had to force himself to hurry.

Ahab had a ride of more than twelve miles that night through this pelting rain. He would have become thoroughly soaked and most uncomfortable. At first this discomfort would have been offset by the sheer joy of seeing it rain at last. As the long miles dragged by, the unpleasantness would have grown and turned to plain misery. The rain beat down relentlessly, stinging his face and making his clothes cold and heavy. However, all this would have added to a most important and forceful impression: Jehovah's prophet had certainly delivered again. As with the fire of the afternoon, so with the water. He had said it would come in a great amount, and surely it did. In truth, Elijah was a remarkable man, and Jehovah was further proved the true God.

But Elijah did yet more to impress the king. "He girded up his loins, and ran before Ahab to the entrance of Jezreel" (v. 46). This was no small feat. The distance was long and it was dark. The pelting rain would have made sight difficult and footing hazardous. To lead prancing horses would have called for good speed besides. It was an achievement to make proud the best of runners. In fact, after a long, tiring day, it was only possible because God supplied special strength, as indicated by the words, "and the hand of Jehovah was on Elijah" (v. 46).

Three matters may have influenced Elijah to make this enormous effort. First, he may have simply wanted to help the king. Elijah knew that Ahab's journey along the Kishon could be difficult as the banks of the river might overflow with the great volume of water. The king might well have needed a guide to show a path over higher ground, which path Elijah may even have scouted ahead of time as a part in his planning. The king's gratitude later on would be of value in the revival. Second, he may have wanted to demonstrate his humility before the king, and so answer any question of Ahab as to Elijah's intentions now that he had received this public acclaim. He was not thinking of revolting against Ahab, but only against Jezebel's religion. And, third, he may have wanted to add to the king's impression of his remarkability as Jehovah's prophet. He had impressed him greatly already—stopping rain, drawing the attention of a worldwide search, bringing miraculous fire, bringing rain once more. Now there he would be again, out there in the darkness, showing the way through the downpour, leading the way to Jezreel. The king would have to extol him the more, and, because of him, Jehovah Whom he served. This, too, should help in the revival contemplated.

Paul bid the Corinthian Christians always to abound in the work of the Lord (1 Cor. 15:58). He instructed Timothy to ". . . be urgent in season, out of season . . ." (2 Tim. 4:2). The extra effort pays off in the business world. Christians should be willing to give it also for God. Elijah did here. He might easily have stopped after praying for the rain. He had put in a long, tiring day by that time. But still he did more, and so much more in this enormous, extra effort. There could be an advantage resulting for the revival, and so he should do it. This was the attitude of which Paul was speaking. It is the attitude God wants us to show. Let us be willing to give the extra for God.

Footnotes to Chapter Nine:

[1]Cf. Deuteronomy 13:6-9; 17:2-7.

[2]*Geshem* and *matar* are used about an equal number of times in the Old Testament, but when a heavy rain is in mind, as with the flood (Gen. 7:12; 8:2), *geshem* is used.

[3]*Hamon* is commonly used to mean "multitude" in respect to people.

[4]First Kings 18:1 does say that God told Elijah it would rain, but that was when Elijah first returned to the land a month before. He did not say when. Elijah could not have known from it that God would send rain this night.

[5]It is significant that James included this statement in the reference we have already considered in other connections, 5:16, 17.

[6]Sisera experienced this with his chariots in his battle with Deborah and Barak (Judg. 4:13-16; 5:20-22).

[7]The expression, "in the meanwhile" (*'adh-coh we'adh-coh*), means literally "unto thus and unto thus," and signifies the interval between two points of time. The one point here would have been when the servant first saw the small cloud, and the other most likely would have been when Ahab started for home.

Chapter Ten

JEZEBEL AND ELIJAH

Jezebel had not been present at the contest. It had been trying enough to have Ahab defy her in arranging it, without personally gracing it. But she had been there in interest. She was, no doubt, waiting for a report when the king reached the palace. We read, "And Ahab told Jezebel all that Elijah had done, and withal how he had slain all the prophets with the sword" (1 Kings 19:1).

A sad commentary is implied respecting the king, for this is all that is stated as to his reaction to this significant day. He had witnessed the clearest evidence as to Who was the true God, but made no changes in view of it. He had seen miraculous fire fall at the call of Jehovah's prophet, and then torrents of rain. Out on the mountain the people had given full committal to Jehovah after only the first of these, yet the king had seen both and gave no new orders. He should have called immediately for a complete return to Jehovah worship, but all he did was relate the day's happenings, stressing the slaying of Jezebel's prophets.

How could a man witness so much and be affected so little? Ahab was an intelligent man. He could evaluate evidence. Without question, in his own thinking there had been impression, as observed. But he kept this to himself, without expressing it to Jezebel or giving orders for change. Perhaps a part of the reason lay in fear of Jezebel. She was ruthless and powerful. He knew he could not control her, and her response would be violent. Another factor could have been a wrong sense of statesmanship, which he felt called for calmness and poise, avoiding radical change. True statesmanship, in the face of issues and demonstrations like these, calls for decisive action. But likely the main reason was simply hardness of heart. He had not changed under prior pressures; he would not now either, in spite of this remarkable demonstration. One is reminded of Abraham's words to the rich man in Hades, "If they hear not Moses and the prophets, neither will they be persuaded, if one rise from the dead" (Luke 16:31). It is easy for us to think that if God would just work some miracle, then people would be convinced. God ordained His Word to be proclaimed by "the foolishness of preaching" (1 Cor. 1:21), and if men do not respond to the oral call, neither will they if miracles are performed.

Jezebel's reaction to these events was yet more deplorable. Ahab, at least, had come home pleased inasmuch as it had rained. But Jezebel was in no way pleased. We read, "Then Jezebel sent a messenger unto Elijah, saying, So let the gods do to me, and more also, if I make not thy life as the life of one of them by to-morrow about this time" (19:2). What a commentary on Jezebel's value as a queen! She displayed no concern for her country. She was not happy about the rain. In fact, we may be sure that she was very unhappy, for now Jehovah would get the credit and not Baal. Her religion had been seriously hurt, with even the prophets now slain. Something drastic had to be done. A good place to begin was with the man responsible, Elijah. She quickly penned a note of warning.

The meaning of her note was clear. She gave added stress to it by a prefaced oath, "gods do to me, and more also, if"[1] which means, "May God punish me even more if this threat is not carried out." The threat was not a small one; she would have Elijah's life, even as he had taken the lives of her prophets, within twenty-four hours.

Elijah's Reaction

Elijah's reaction is succinctly stated: "And when he saw that, he arose, and went for his life . . ." (v. 3). Likely the note arrived yet that night, for Jezebel would have wasted no time. Likely, too, Elijah fled that night, for he could not have known what time she might send the swordsman. Neither Elijah nor his servant received the rest which they needed so badly after the exhausting day. Dawn found them walking in haste along the road already some distance south of Jezreel.

Was the prophet right in this action? Was it God's will that he flee? Some have argued that it was, pointing out, for instance, that Jezebel, ruthless as she was, would not have hesitated to carry out her warning, and Elijah would have been no use to the revival then. Argument also has been taken from the loving care God extended to Elijah shortly after, down in the desert (vv. 5-7). Would God have been this gracious if He were displeased that Elijah had run? Still further, it has been asked if a man of such courage, as displayed by Elijah earlier that same day, could have lost that courage in so short a time, as would be true if he were fleeing out of God's will.

Though one would like to be convinced by these arguments, the evidence is all too clear that Elijah indeed was wrong, and tragically so. He had conducted himself so well until this point, providing a shining example of strength and faith as we have seen; but here he failed. When he ran that night, he did nothing less than take all chance for revival with him. Until then, the prospects for real change had been good. As we have seen, the contest on Mount Carmel could hardly have worked better. The people had given their full committal, both in word and decisive action. As a result, this large group of leaders stood ready that night to give complete cooperation, their positions and lives depending on it. Still no revival came. There was one main reason: Elijah ran.

A brief consideration shows why. When Elijah had left the scene of victory on Mount Carmel, the fifteen hundred followers had looked to him both as a symbol and director of the revival. They had expected continued dramatic action, such as the destruction of Baal altars, slaying of Asherah prophets, and even deposition of Jezebel. They had been ready to help in this action. Accordingly, they would have experienced crushing disillusionment when they learned he had run. He who had been their champion, who had seemed so invincible, who had provided them real hope for success, had fled himself when confronted by the queen. All spirit for revival would immediately have died. If their leader had not dared to stand, then how could they? With hope for revival gone, fear for personal safety would have set in. Because they had helped in slaying Jezebel's prophets, she could have them treated similarly in a short time. What could they do to save their own lives?

What did happen in the next few days may be safely conjectured. Jezebel would have spared no effort to exploit the fact that Elijah had run. In her own version, she would have spread the story far and wide by whatever means available. Then she would have begun to seek out the ones who had cooperated on Mount Carmel. They were dangerous persons. If she was to bring her country under solid control again, they would have to be eliminated. Maybe Ahab intervened to stop this; it would be nice to think so. If he did not, surely she would have carried it out. She had not hesitated in slaying the prophets of Jehovah; thus she would not have drawn back here. She would not have been satisfied until she had removed all factions advocating change.

This reason of spoiling the revival is alone sufficient to show that Elijah was in error in running, but there are more reasons. One is that Jezebel did not want to take Elijah's life anyway. What she wanted was exactly what he did: he ran. Had she wanted his life, she would not have given him warning. She would have sent an executioner, not a messenger. We may be sure that she had not given advance notice to the Jehovah prophets. Nor had Elijah himself given the Baal prophets that very afternoon any warning. He did not want them to escape; he wanted their lives. Moreover, if Jezebel took Elijah's life, he could become a martyr symbol to his followers and this could yet ignite the revival fire. He should be made to run. This would destroy all incentive, leaving fear and despair in its place.

Another is found in God's twice-spoken question to Elijah later on Mount Horeb, far to the south: "What doest thou here, Elijah?" (vv. 9, 13). This is the first word recorded which God spoke to the prophet following his flight. Why was Elijah down at Horeb? He did not belong there, but up in Israel where revival was supposed to be in progress. Why had he run when all had been proceeding so well? Why was he not back leading the revival? God was plainly showing His displeasure at Elijah's action.

Two lessons come to us in view of this tragic mistake. One is a lesson of comfort. Christians, prone to err in God's service, need not think themselves alone in their weakness. They have company, including men of great spiritual stature. Even Elijah fell. This does not give reason for self-satisfaction. One should not rejoice, but only grieve. It is a help to know that one is not alone. Then, too, it is a comfort to know that Elijah was not cast aside because of his error, serious as it was. God reinstated him to service after giving appropriate admonition and instruction.[2] It is normal for God to do the same today.

The other is a lesson of warning. If such a great servant as Elijah could fall so seriously, then so can we. No one, no matter how spiritually strong, can afford to think himself immune. How often we find ourselves tending to do this very thing, however, showing pride in our Christian maturity! This very pride itself can lead quickly to the fall. Satan is powerful and crafty and uses every means available. Even Elijah was not above his wiles.

Why Did Elijah Run?

What prompted Elijah to run and make this tragic mistake? Was it merely fear or were there other factors? He had been so courageous out on Mount Carmel; how could he have changed this radically in a few hours? The following matters are suggested in the story.

1. He Was Tired Physically

Elijah was too exhausted physically to make a proper decision. If he had waited until morning, he may have decided differently. There is close relation between mental and physical health. A worried mind can produce a sick body, and a sick body can cause an anxious mind. A rested body lends a sense of confidence. A sick body tends toward melancholy and depression. Problems loom large when one is tired; and decisions made then can easily be wrong.

Elijah was extremely tired by the time he reached Jezreel that night. Even the days prior to the contest had been taxing, for he had worked to stimulate interest and make preparations. The day itself especially called for all his energy. The responsibility had been great simply in taking the lead at all times, particularly before so many important people and the enemy prophets. He had given the opening instructions and then the noon-hour mockery, not being sure as to the possible response. Later, he had called the people to witness his attempt, and though his confidence had been strong, fatiguing tension would have been there. How would the people react when the fire fell? How would they react when he ordered the slaying of the opposing prophets? God had permitted the extra anxiety too of not answering the prayer for rain through six times of petition. Finally, there was the twelve-mile run to Jezreel, an enormous effort to challenge

112

even the best-trained man fresh at the start. Truly Elijah was completely exhausted when Jezebel's note arrived, too tired to cope with the problem it presented. His mind was not quick to see the significance that it was a note and not a sword; or to recognize that God would never let a mere queen stop a revival that God had planned so long and which was already progressing so well. Had he waited until morning, after a night of good rest, he may well have decided differently.[3]

2. He Was Alone in This Decision

Another matter is that Elijah was alone when he made this decision. He had no companion with whom to consult or examine implications. His servant was probably there, but he was likely a hindrance rather than a help. He had not been with the prophet long,[4] and he was left behind at Beersheba shortly thereafter (v. 3). He certainly was not of Elijah's spiritual stature and so would have urged the flight rather than counseled against it. Elijah's need was for a fellow prophet who could understand, sympathize and help analyze Jezebel's thinking. But he had none. He was alone as well as exhausted. If he had had a real confidant, again the choice may have been different.[5]

In this light, it is significant that one of God's directives to Elijah later on Mount Horeb, prior to his return to service, was to find such a helper. God said, ". . . And Elisha the son of Shaphat of Abel-meholah shalt thou anoint to be prophet in thy room" (v. 16). Elisha was to be with him. The text says that he was to be Elijah's successor, rather than be with him, but we know that he also accompanied him all during his remaining years of ministry.[6] Apparently God recognized that Elijah had this need of a helper and so supplied it.

3. He Liked the Dramatic But Not the Routine

A third matter is that Elijah naturally liked dramatic action, but not routine and tedium. He found it easier to work for big movements, affecting many people at once, rather than slow, plodding contact with individuals. For this reason, he had planned well for the contest, but not for follow-up activity, nor for eventualities such as this note. He should have looked ahead and anticipated all possible developments. If he had, he would not have been taken back this way by Jezebel's message. Certainly he would not have run.

Evidence that Elijah was emotionally constituted in this way is not hard to find. Mount Carmel presented the quintessence of dramatic activity. Here was the contest, the large crowd, important people and an assured defeat of Baal. Here would come evidence that could turn the whole country in one sweep to Jehovah. And here Elijah performed masterfully. He gave the orders, voiced the mockery, caught the imagination of the people and drew their full committal. There was no thought of defeat or running here. Forty-two months earlier he had been in a similar dramatic situation. He had already prayed for rainless years, something certainly to affect the whole country at once. Then he went directly to Ahab, showing again great courage in telling the king that no rain would fall. He made his entrance, gave the message and withdrew, all with finesse and poise. No thought of running was apparent.

Further evidence is found in God's later instructions to Elijah on Mount Horeb (19:11, 12). There God taught him through a tremendous object lesson of wind, earthquake and fire, and these followed by "a still small voice." The full significance of this occasion will be viewed later,[7] but one clear lesson was God's rejection of big things for small. Each time of wind, earthquake or fire, it is stated that God was not in it. God was thus admonishing His prophet that big and dramatic actions do not constitute His normal method of operation. Elijah had thought so and needed correction. Because of this he had not planned further than the contest itself, but somehow had thought that it alone would suffice. The revival should develop then almost of itself. He was not ready to meet an unexpected feature such as Jezebel's note.

4. *He Had a Tendency To Be Proud*

It has been observed that when Elijah prayed for rain he displayed commendable humility. It was also observed, however, that the reason God let him wait seven times before answering was that he had a tendency to be proud. This tendency also contributed to the wrong decision. Before noting in what way, however, we look at other evidences that Elijah had to combat pride.

One comes in his request to God in the southern desert: "It is enough; now, O Jehovah, take away my life; for I am not better than my fathers" (v. 4). The implication here is that Elijah had thought he would do more than his predecessors. He would effect the revival that they had not. He would outshine them. Because he had not, he was now ready to die. Such thinking comes from a proud heart.

Two other evidences come from his repeated reply to God's question on Mount Horeb as to why he was there:

> I have been very jealous for Jehovah, the God of hosts; for the children of Israel have forsaken thy covenant, thrown down thine altars, and slain thy prophets with the sword; and I, even I only, am left; and they seek my life, to take it away (vv. 10, 14).

Elijah was justifying his action in running. He had been right in all that he had done, but had lacked help. No one had stood with him, and he had been forced to run.

One indication of pride here is that this was an attempt at self-justification. The person who does this invariably is trying to protect himself and make others think better of him than his actions warrant. This is what Obadiah had done before Elijah, and now Elijah was doing the same before God. Another indication is that Elijah even resorted to an inaccurate statement to make this self-justification more convincing. He said that no persons in Israel followed Jehovah any longer. This made his case stronger, if true, but it was not. We know that fifteen hundred had given their committal on Mount Carmel;[8] and, further, God told Elijah directly that there were seven thousand who had "not bowed unto Baal" (19:18). Elijah's inaccuracy here can be understood only in terms of a highly confused mind, of which more will be said later, and a heart that was proud.

One way in which this tendency towards pride would have influenced Elijah's decision is that it would have contributed to his placing too great a reliance on the Mount Carmel contest, as already observed. He would plan so well and effect so efficiently that little else would be needed. Another is that pride would have kept him from admitting that he had been wrong in this thinking. As a result, when the contest alone proved insufficient, as shown by Jezebel's note, his mind had refused to consider other alternatives, believing that nothing else could work either. A third way, and the most serious, is that pride would have hindered Elijah in asking for God to reveal His will in respect to the decision. Certainly God would have told him if he had asked, but Elijah did not ask.

If such items as these—being tired, being alone, liking the dramatic and being proud—could make a man of Elijah's stature commit this tragic error, they could do the same for us. We do well to take notice and warning. It is never wise to make important decisions when tired. Late-at-night choices, after a weary day, should be avoided. A fresh mind weighs evidence much more accurately. Problems can be viewed in a much truer light. Then it is good to have a helper, an assistant, a confidant, one with whom to share burdens. Fullest abilities are realized through fellowship and interchange. A wife can play an invaluable role. A fellow servant of God can lend helpful counsel. Further, one should discipline himself for the routine aspects of God's work as well as, and for the most part in place of, the sensational and dramatic. This is not easy, for the routine is slow and often uninteresting. But God works normally in the framework of the "still small voice." It should also be said that one need not be discouraged when great accomplishments are not seen. If one is faithful in doing the work that God has given, he need never be disheartened. He can trust God to bring the fruit in His own time. Finally, pride should be resisted vigorously and continually. This is the most difficult of all. Pride comes so easily and without recognition. In pride lies one of. the greatest dangers for all God's work. It is a principal tool of Satan in bringing defeat and error into Christian lives; thus we must be on our guard at all times.

Footnotes to Chapter Ten:

[1]For discussion regarding oaths, *supra*, p. 18.

[2]Given on Mount Horeb, *infra*, pp. 129-136.

[3]It is significant that God's first provision for him following this time was rest and food. He needed both to restore his energy (vv. 5-8).

[4]First mentioned as with him on Mount Carmel (18:43). Likely Elijah had enlisted him especially for help in the contest.

[5]It may be that Elijah's stress on aloneness in his repeated words to God on Mount Horeb (vv. 10, 14) was in part due psychologically to his having been alone in this decision.

[6]They may have been together as many as ten years. Elijah outlived Ahab and the two-year reign of his first son, Ahaziah, being taken to heaven in the early part of Jehoram's rule (2 Kings 2). In Ahab's reign there was time at least for three important battles with the Syrians (1 Kings 20, 22), and the first of these could not have followed directly after the famine for both countries would have had to recover from its affects.

[7]*Infra*, pp. 128-136.

[8]It may be that Jezebel had killed most, if not all, of these by this time, but Elijah would have had no way of knowing this. He may have surmised it, but this would not have justified him in making this flat statement to God. Also, Elijah must have known such a fearless prophet as Micaiah who, a few years later (1 Kings 22), withstood Ahab's four hundred false prophets so courageously.

117

Chapter Eleven

ELIJAH IN THE DESERT

One sin so often leads to another and it was so with Elijah. He soon wanted to die, saying, "It is enough; now, O Jehovah, take away my life . . ." (1 Kings 19:4). This request was voiced in the desert south of Beersheba, but it had been in his mind when he left this city for he had taken neither food nor water with him. He had also left his servant there.

What led Elijah to this frame of mind? When he had left Jezreel, he had run to save his life. Now he wanted to lose it. The change had come as he had walked south toward Judah. He had run first without reflection; natural instinct had prompted a desire for safety. As he walked he realized that he really had no place to go and be of use. He could not return to Israel, and he could not stop in Judah either, for diplomatic propriety would call for King Jehoshaphat to return him to Israel.[1] Beyond was only desert, and of what good to God could he be there? It would be best if God would take his life.

But Elijah was out of God's will in this desire. God made this clear in not granting the request but providing sustaining food instead. He had work for Elijah to do, as He would soon show him on Mount Horeb. Elijah had not consulted God as to this request to die. He had acted purely out of his own will.

118

Elijah sinned also in not consulting God in respect to any aspect of his flight. He had not sought guidance before he fled, as we have seen, nor did he as he traveled. The whole tenor of the story and his manner of action give evidence that he did not. This was not like Elijah. Always before he had moved only as God had directed. Even though he had run that night under the pressures we have seen, he should have recovered his spiritual balance the following day. God would have heard. If it had already been too late to return, He would have told him what was best now. Certainly, then, Elijah would not have found himself down in the desert a few days later pitifully crying for death, without food or water. It is easy to get one's self into difficult and unpleasant situations when one does not look to God for direction.

Elijah's further sin in this can only have been as a subconscious result of having first run without due consultation. He had thus put himself in a position of self-defense against God in having to argue the necessity of his flight.[2] Self-defense against God does not lead to consultation with God. This means that Elijah was a man out of fellowship. He had sinned grievously and was now caught in consequent entanglements. It would take time and even God's gracious admonition on Mount Horeb to reinstate the former close communion. Christians often find themselves similarly entangled. A first sin leads to another and suddenly one finds himself far from God. Fellowship is gone, joy has departed and life is miserable. Days of waste and defeat set in; mental depression descends. It is so important to resist the first sin that leads to this God-displeasing state. It is also important, if one finds himself becoming thus entangled, to turn quickly to God in humble prayer for forgiveness that restoration may be made. It would have been so much better if Elijah had prayed the very next day after he had run.

Elijah's Need

God did not grant Elijah's request for death. Instead, He gently rebuked him by providing food to keep him alive. It will be of help in understanding the full significance of this provision to consider first the extent and nature of Elijah's needs.

His physical needs were rest and nourishment, as we have seen. He needed these badly. He had been extremely fatigued when he began the flight, and since that time had traveled, by forced march, at least a hundred miles.[3] He had rested some along the way, but always with the urge to press on. This means that his exhaustion in the desert was even greater than at Jezreel. And food, of course, had remained a constant problem. Water supply had improved since the big rain, but not food. We may be sure that Elijah had eaten next to nothing since the day of the contest.

Furthermore, Elijah's needs were more than physical. He also had emotional and spiritual needs which were of still greater import. What is revealed concerning him in the desert shows a soul deeply disturbed. One contributing factor was the fear that he had experienced as he fled. We read that he had run "for his life" (19:3). A degree of panic had been involved, and panic is shattering to one's emotional balance. There was little chance of further pursuit down in the desert, but still the effects would have lingered.

Then there was despondency over his apparent failure. Revival efforts had been expended over no less than forty-two months, and now they had ended with nothing accomplished. The hosts of Baal were supposed to be in flight, but instead he was. In place of Jehovah worship being restored, the Baal program unquestionably was being entrenched more firmly than ever. He had reviewed the reasons over and over, but had found nothing to bring consolation. Somehow he had failed.

And, still further, there was the serious, subconscious

conflict with God already observed. This estrangement was new. He had always been able to draw near to God, no matter how trying the circumstances. When doubts had assailed, God had been there to reassure. Now this closeness was gone. Instead, he found himself arguing against God, justifying his action. The more he did this, the further removed God's presence seemed to be. He missed the fellowship sorely, but still found it impossible to cease arguing. Thus the conflict remained.

God's Provision

Perhaps no moment in all of Elijah's life was to prove more tender in his memory than this occasion in the desert when God graciously met these needs. Other moments would also prove precious, but this time God provided for him while yet disobedient and unwilling to repent. The blessing came, not because of Elijah's actions, but altogether in spite of them. This was grace indeed.

The physical provisions suited the requirements exactly—sleep for fatigue and food and water for nourishment. Elijah first slept, after making his request to die. Then he was awakened by an angel and told to eat. He was permitted again to sleep and then reawakened to eat. No command was needed that he sleep. Being so tired, this was natural. But he also needed to eat and this called for intervention to awaken him.

The food was before him each time he awoke. He needed only to appropriate it. God provided it miraculously for there was no food in the vicinity otherwise. This was the third time that God intervened to provide His prophet sustenance. The first at Cherith, by means of ravens, and the second at Zarephath, by means of non-depleting food containers, had been of a semi-permanent type, each lasting for many months. This was only temporary. All were supernatural in origin, however. This time, water was present in a jug and a cake lay "baken on the coals" (v. 6).

The phrase "baken on the coals"[4] suggests that the cake was warm. The "coals" were right there. This means that the provision this time was even better than at Cherith. It may have reminded Elijah more of Zarephath where the first cake had also been warm; in fact, it was mixed and baked for him as he waited. This one was warm. What tenderness this showed on God's part! He not only supplied him food, but fresh and warm food! If the cake was so presented, it follows that the water too was especially cool and refreshing. God, in truth, was being gracious.

Several aspects in this provision would have ministered also to Elijah's emotional and spiritual needs. The first is simply that God provided at all when Elijah was so undeserving. He could have left Elijah quite alone. Elijah was out of fellowship with God, and he knew it. For this reason he had not expected this consideration. Yet here it was, and the significance would not have been missed. God was still interested in him. The second is that the provision was made through the medium of a personal emissary. Food was not only made available, but an angel was commissioned to serve it! This was unusual attention. History does not record many instances of personal angelic appearances and Elijah himself had not been granted this experience before. But here was an angel ministering to him, and he so undeserving of any favor at all![5]

Recognition of these two facts alone should have done much to restore Elijah's spirit. They showed that God had not cast him off after all. He was still with him to provide his needs, and even in this special way. This was real reason for encouragement.

But this was not all. A third aspect, negative in kind this time, is that God completely omitted any mention of Elijah's sin in running. No rebuke was administered. One could have expected it. Forty-two months of invested effort were fruitless because this man had sinned. Elijah certainly

122

was deserving of the severest reprimand. However, nothing was said; not here at least. The reason can only be that God did not wish at this time to add to Elijah's despondency. He needed encouragement now, not added emotional turmoil. There would be time later for rebuke.

A fourth aspect, again positive, is that God implied encouragement for Elijah in the repeated words of the angel, "Arise and eat" (vv. 5, 7). This indicated that there was reason yet for Elijah to live. Rebuke was involved in this inasmuch as he had asked to die, as we have seen, but there was also promise that God still had use for him. That the food was provided in such an appetizing condition carried further significance. God surely was favoring him and so was interested in him.

A fifth aspect is that God implied similar encouragement in the angel's closing words: "The journey is too great for thee" (v. 7). From this Elijah could know that God had a journey in mind for him. This meant a destination and purpose. Elijah had not known where to go as he had walked south earlier, and this had contributed to his despondency; but God had some place in view for him. There must be a reason for him to live.

Noting these provisions, tailor-made to Elijah's needs, we must be impressed again with the wisdom and grace of God. He knew Elijah's needs better than Elijah himself and He met them, both physical and spiritual. Even where unusual grace was called for, He was willing to give it. If particularly appetizing food would help, or a special messenger would add to the blessing, these were not too much to supply. His servant, though having sinned, was in need of special consideration. God loves His children. He delights in providing for them. The provision comes sometimes in unexpected ways, but it is always right and good. It is wonderful to be His child.

Some might ask why God did not send Elijah back to

Israel at this time rather than waiting until after the Mount Horeb encounter. The answer is that there was no longer reason for hurry, it being too late to effect the revival. In fact, there was reason not to hurry, for Jezebel certainly was bringing havoc upon all revival sympathizers and likely would not any longer have hesitated in taking Elijah's life. Besides this, both reprimand and instruction were in order for Elijah. He had sinned and needed rebuke; and with further work to do back in Israel, he needed information. Both would be given on Mount Horeb.

As Elijah walked along following his meeting with the angel, he was already quite a different man. Before he had been completely defeated, but now he had reason to live. Relief from fatigue and hunger alone would have done much. Even more important would have been the knowledge that God was still with him, having ministered to him through an angel. No rebuke had been administered, and in its place prospect for usefulness had been implied. He still could not see that he had been wrong in running, however, and continued to justify himself. This kept him from repenting and having full fellowship restored. But he was now able to think more clearly and so be in suitable form to profit from what God had in mind for him ahead.

Footnotes to Chapter Eleven:

[1]Especially so since the marriage of Jehoram, his son, and Athaliah, daughter of Ahab and Jezebel, had likely taken place not long before (2 Kings 8:16-29). The son of Jehoram and Athaliah, Ahaziah, was twenty-two when he began to reign. Taking this date as 841 B.C., he was born in 863 B.C., which means the marriage of Jehoram and Athaliah was no later than 864 B.C., or about ten years prior to Ahab's death, the approximate time of the beginning of the famine in Israel.

[2]He was still arguing this necessity on Mount Horeb one month later. Cf. 19:10, 14.

[3]It is approximately ninety-five miles from Jezreel to Beersheba by straight line. This means that his line of walk would have been over a hundred miles.

[4]The phrase, "cake baken on the coals," is literally, "cake of baking stones." Such a cake was baked by placing it on flat stones heated by ashes or live coals. There would be little point in the text speaking of a cake of "baking stones" if the stones were not yet hot for such baking.

[5]One can believe that Elijah would have had difficulty, in spite of his fatigue, in returning to sleep after actually seeing an angel if the angel had remained there. However, in that it says, "And the angel of Jehovah came again the second time . . ." (v. 7), it appears that the angel disappeared after the first speaking.

Chapter Twelve

ELIJAH ON MOUNT HOREB

Elijah's journey led to Mount Horeb, a distance of about two hundred miles. Taking forty days, when ten should have sufficed, the prophet certainly did not walk fast, and probably not directly. He may not even have had this destination in mind, but just some place other than back north to Israel. However, he would have known of Mount Horeb as the "mount of God"[1] where God had met Moses and Israel many centuries earlier, and so could have been subconsciously drawn this way, desiring the same contact for himself.

The text says that he went in "the strength of" (1 Kings 19:8) the food which the angel had supplied for the entire forty days. This means that he had eaten well at the time, but it also means that God provided special strength besides. Elijah could not have eaten enough to last so long and he must have become very hungry along the way. God might have sent the angel again to feed him, but He did not. This means that God wanted him to become hungry, and the question arises as to why. The answer can only be that God saw it as most conducive to making Elijah a proper recipient for what was in store for him on Mount Horeb. He needed to be made humble and teachable, and it is a lack of life's provisions which works to this end and not plenty. One is caused then to throw himself more on God's mercy, recognizing his own insufficiency. Tending otherwise to be proud, Elijah would have been made more pliable and receptive.

Upon arriving at the mountain, Elijah took up residence in a cave.[2] There God broke the long silence by the deeply probing question, "What doest thou here, Elijah?" (v. 9). As observed earlier,[3] God was telling Elijah that he had erred in leaving Israel and did not belong at Horeb. This was the first indication to this effect that Elijah had received. The prophet had persisted in his self-justification, and doubtless had taken encouragement from the absence of any reprimand from God. But here was correction. God was challenging the fact that he was down at Mount Horeb.

Elijah's immediate response was to argue back. He had continued too long in this thinking to desist quickly. He had been "very jealous for Jehovah" (v. 10), but the people had been wrong in forsaking God's covenant, breaking His altars and slaying His prophets. There had been no recourse but to run. When God voiced the question again, after the intervening nature display (v. 13), Elijah still answered the same, indicating how deeply his previous thinking had been engrained. Change did not come easily.

A practical truth should be noted respecting the extended silence of God concerning Elijah's great error. Elijah took this as approval of his action, but it was really only a display of God's patience. God's children may never assume that His silence means His approval. At times God may even permit one to continue for a long while in a wayward and blundering manner before speaking. This is not approval. God had not approved Elijah's action. Elijah had assumed so because he continued to justify himself. But he had been wrong. What a tremendous shock it must have been when the truth was finally realized! He had erred! The reason for the failure was found in himself! The revival had not come because he had run!

The Great Object Lesson

In between the first and second statements of the question, God effected an object lesson of enormous proportions. No words of explanation were spoken during its enactment. It was simply a wordless object lesson for Elijah to observe. It was not for his entertainment either, but from it he was to learn lessons. It consisted of three tremendous displays of natural forces, followed by a contrasting "still small voice."

The first display was of wind so strong that it "rent the mountains, and brake in pieces the rocks" (v. 11). Only wind of tornado force could do this. The mountains evidently were made to vibrate so that boulders were dislodged and caused to crash downward, splitting as they went. The sound would have been deafening. Elijah, who had been told to come out from his cave far enough to see, would have tended to move back at the awesome sight.

The second display was an earthquake. No indication of intensity is given this time, leaving the implication that it was the same as with the wind. This means that the mountain, which had just ceased vibrating from the wind, now began to do so more violently than before. Landslides would have formed and made even more noise. Seams would have opened on the mountainside, perhaps rather near the prophet. It is said that few experiences bring terror like an earthquake when the earth moves beneath one's feet. Elijah's emotional disturbances this time would have been greater than the first.

Thirdly came fire. Again a commensurate power is implied. There would have been little to burn in the desert, especially after such a violent wind, but God does not need fuel for fire. The fire Moses had seen on this same mountain years before had not consumed the bush on which it burned. Even so, it had been real fire, as this was real—live, leaping, glowing fire. The wind and earthquake had dimmed the light with flying debris, but this brought a contrasting bright light. It also brought heat to drive the prophet farther back into the cave. It too would have stirred him deeply, as he strove to find the meaning of it all.

He was probably bracing himself for the next onslaught when, in complete contrast, there came the "still small voice." Whether this "voice" was a speaking voice, stating some unidentified message, or only a clear, quiet sound, is not indicated.[4] In either case, it was totally different from what had been before. The contrast would have been the thing which affected him this time.

All this was for the purpose of admonishing and instructing the prophet, as has been observed. Lessons that did not need explanation but poignant illustration needed to be taught. The subject matter is made clear by God's pivotal question, used both as introduction and conclusion: "What doest thou here, Elijah?" At least five lessons were intended.

1. God's Power

The first concerns a fresh impression on Elijah of the greatness of God's power. That the awesome display consisted of three tremendous forces of nature is significant of this. Nothing impresses man more forcibly as to power than control of nature. The disciples had seen Jesus perform many miracles previously, but it was only when He had stilled raging wind and waves on the Sea of Galilee that they cried out, "What manner of man is this?"[5] They had seen Jesus feed over five thousand persons with but five loaves and two fish on an afternoon, but it was only after He had walked on water and again stilled contrary wind that "they were sore amazed in themselves," for they had not considered the miracle of the "loaves."[6]

Elijah, witnessing these three marked manipulations in nature, could not have avoided a renewed impression of God's great power. He not only saw wind made to cease, as the disciples, but first made to start; then the same for earthquake, and the same for fire. He actually saw six times as much nature control as had so impressed the disciples. With such stress on power, it is clear that in this lay one of God's intentions.

Why did Elijah need to be impressed with God's power? Did he not know it already? In fact, had he not drawn on that power in unusual degree many times before—withholding rain, raising the widow's child, calling down fire? Yes, but somehow the reality of that power had become dim by the time Jezebel's note arrived the night of the flight. He had not acted in terms of it then. He had run as if God could not protect him. And in his cold, self-justifying condition since, there had been no return of that reality. For this reason, renewal was necessary. Thus God gave it. God was saying, "Elijah, you did not need to run that night for this is how powerful I am. I could have protected you no matter what Jezebel might have tried to do, employing even a tornado, earthquake or fire."[7]

Elijah's choice would have been different that night if the reality of God's power had been fresh in his mind. He would not have run. If he had not, what a difference for Israel there would have been! Revival would have come! A similar difference will result in the lives of all God's people as they experience a fresh recognition of God's power daily. God is as great today as He was then, but there needs to be a continual awareness of this greatness. It is one thing to know about God's power abstractly, but it is another to know it concretely, and think and plan one's life in view of it. Daily reminder is needed because it is easy to forget, even as did Elijah.

2. God's Power Is Present

The second lesson is that this power was present and available for Elijah personally. The prophet's recognition of this intended truth would have come from this nature display being effected for himself alone. He was the only spectator. He could not look around and wonder who God had in mind to impress. This was for his own benefit. The demonstration rated an enormous audience. Never in all history had such a display of power been portrayed. Nevertheless, a great crowd was not present; only Elijah. God was showing that His power, in even such quantity as this, was available personally to His servant.

Elijah had known this truth before. He had acted on it many times. But the recognition somehow had dimmed by that sad night. God's power had seemed far away as he had read Jezebel's note. God was now telling him that it had not been far away. It had been available; not only great enough to do the job, but available. Even as it was here at hand to stir up tornado, earthquake and fire, so it had been at hand that night to do as much. Elijah had not needed to run.

Here, too, is a precious note of counsel and comfort for any day. God is always present with His children. His power is not just for someone, some place, under some conditions; but for one's self, in his own place, under his conditions. God knows each personally and cares. He knows every individual need. God was with Elijah that night, as it were, reading the note along with him. He knew what it said. Elijah was taken back, but not God. He knew just what to do to counter Jezebel's plan. If it called for a tornado, earthquake or fire, He was ready to supply it. He knows the need of every Christian. He knows when the frightening letter arrives, the note of dismissal from work, the news of accident, sickness or death. He knows, cares and will supply.

3. God's High Evaluation of One Man's Service[8]

The third lesson is that God places high value on the sacrifice of each man for himself. He expended enormous effort here to refit for service one man only, Elijah. Sometimes the child of God shrugs off God's personal call with the thought that others are available; thus he thinks his own response is not so important. God has a task for each and wants each, not someone else, to assume it.

We could think that God might have taken someone else here rather than Elijah. Elisha, whom Elijah was soon to summon anyway, was ready for service. Micaiah was also active and available. The point is, God did not have them in mind. There was reason too for not recalling Elijah. He had failed seriously. He had fled just when revival was ready to break. He had spoiled nothing less than forty-two months of preparation. Had he not forfeited all right to further consideration? No, God still wanted Elijah, and enough to expend this amount of effort—providing food in the desert and here even wind, earthquake and fire.

God's call should never be taken lightly. When He calls, He wants the one He calls. Each of His tasks has, as it were, a name on it. God wants that person to perform it. It may be a Sunday school class, a church office or a life's call to the ministry. The one whom God has in mind for each task, He wants to fulfill it.

4. God Usually Works in Small Ways, Not Big

In the first three lessons, the power display has been the center of interest. With the last two, the attention turns to the contrast made by the "still small voice." The contrast is stressed in the story. Repetition is made in respect to each of the nature demonstrations that "Jehovah was not in" it. The implication is clear that He was in the "still small voice." This indicated a clear rejection of big things for small. God was saying "no" to great power procedures and "yes" to something quiet and still. This "no" and "yes" contrast brings lessons four and five.

The fourth is that God was saying "no" to the big and dramatic way of doing His work and "yes" to the small and unobtrusive; that Elijah should no longer think of the sensational means of bringing revival, but rather of simple contact with the few here and there.[9] Elijah's approach thus far had been only to use the big and dramatic. He had first prayed for nothing less than famine, and later proceeded with the great Mount Carmel contest.[10] He had thought in terms of this contest accomplishing all in one grand movement. When this did not happen, he was ready to quit and die, thus indicating how much he had depended on the big. He had thought that if the big did not prove effective, then nothing else was worth considering.[11] But he had been wrong. God usually works in quite different ways than famine and contest. His more normal effort is with the few here and there, persuading through simple preaching. And this was His message to the prophet. Both rebuke and instruction were involved. Elijah had been wrong in thinking he had tried everything worthwhile when he had used only the big; he was now to begin with the small, which was God's usual method.

Tying in with this lesson is God's mention in verse 18 that there were yet seven thousand who had not bowed to Baal. This was partly to correct Elijah's statement that he alone remained, but it was yet more a part of Elijah's reassignment. God was saying that these seven thousand needed a pastor, a shepherd, to give instruction and encouragement under a most cruel regime. Elijah was to seek these people out and give them the help they needed when he returned. This means that his task was to be twofold: trying to persuade others to turn to Jehovah, and so continue his earlier efforts, only now with the small approach; and caring for these who already had decided for the true God. Elijah would be busy in his new ministry.

Looking ahead into the days that followed, there is reason to believe that he did what God told him, and unusually well. We read no more of rainless years, nor of great contests.[12] In fact, we read little of Elijah at all, though he continued to serve some ten years. This is what we should expect. This was a ministry much more normal for prophets which did not draw headlines or particular notices. The most significant indication comes from the wonderful tribute God paid him when the quiet work had been completed. Elijah did not have to die, but was caught home to Heaven in a "chariot of fire" (2 Kings 2:11). That which called for this high honor could hardly have been Elijah's work prior to Mount Horeb, in view of his terrible failure in running. It must have been mainly this "still small voice" ministry of reaching the few and caring for the seven thousand.

Big movements and sweeping revivals have their place in the work of God. God is pleased when large numbers of people turn to Him and He would have been pleased had all Israel turned to Him after Mount Carmel. He was in this big operation, having planned it through Elijah. But this is not God's usual way. Far more common is the smaller movement, the working with a few. Scripture does not often record nationwide efforts, but many times the turning of the few through faithful preaching.[13] God puts a high premium on faithfulness, no matter the size of the task. It is sometimes harder to do the unnoticed than that which achieves headlines. It is important to be faithful and show courage wherever God makes an assignment. He will reward accordingly.

5. God Is Longsuffering in Vindication

The fifth lesson is that God desired to be gentle in His treatment of Jezebel and Israel, rather than vindictive. He was saying "no" to what undoubtedly had come to be Elijah's thinking during his prior forty-day walk; namely, if revival still was to be effected, there was one main thing needful and that was the slaying of Jezebel.

Evidence of this thinking is revealed in Elijah's repeated response to God. This response indicated a self-pitying mind full of resentment for others and especially Jezebel. She had sent the note that night and had been the one who previously had broken Jehovah's altars and slain His prophets. If it had not been for her, revival would have come. From her he himself had had to flee and he did not care to think of what she might have done to those who had stood with him on Mount Carmel. There was one answer to revival and that was to get rid of her. Take her life as she had taken the lives of so many others.

This thinking by Elijah was what had called for the particular kind of power portrayal God used in this great object lesson. If the intention had been to impress the prophet only with power in general, God might have used other means. But He chose destructive forces. Elijah would be shown what might be done to rid the land of Jezebel, but then be told each time, "No, this is not the way." The "yes" would come only with the gentle voice. He must learn that God's way was not by vengeance.

Elijah's reaction as each form of destruction was presented is not hard to imagine. He would have been delighted. Anyone of these would be just fine and would accomplish what he had been thinking exactly. Along with his terror, then, would have been a real sense of satisfaction. God was agreeing with him that the queen must be destroyed. However, as each form was successively turned down as the particular way, and then the affirmation implied instead to the gentle voice, this satisfaction would have vanished and Elijah would have felt the rebuke God intended. Elijah had been wrong. God was not planning to destroy Jezebel after all. He intended to be gentle and patient with her.

It will be shown presently that God's reassignment directions (19:15-18) also find rationale in this same lesson thought. God's word to Elijah now was a firm "no" to vengeance, but it would not always be. There would come a time when patience would no longer be in order, but retaliation. That would be when the two kings, Jehu and Hazael, would be anointed to rule over their respective countries. They would wield their swords (v. 17) and bring the necessary punishment on Jezebel, her court and the nation generally. For now, however, Elijah was to return to the land and simply be a normal prophet—preaching, counseling and comforting—and forget about this matter of vindication.

It is not easy to leave vengeance to God.[14] We want to bring it ourselves. We want to pay back, get even, bring reprisal. But because we do, we cause harm. Misunderstandings erupt into quarrels, and quarrels into serious damage to the work of God. It is not easy to be patient, but this is God's way. He says, "Vengeance is mine; I will repay" (Rom. 12: 19, KJV). When He repays, it is done right; where it is due, it is in just measure.

Reassignment Instructions

God's reassignment instructions to Elijah are puzzling at first. They consisted only in directions to anoint three people to office: Hazael as king of Syria, Jehu as king of Israel and Elisha as a prophet. He said nothing as to the day by day ministry Elijah was to perform when he returned, where or how it was to be done. Further, two of these anointings Elijah himself would not be able to effect for he would be dead before they would be possible.

The reason for these unusual features is found in the fact, as just indicated, that God was continuing instruction relative to the "vengeance" lesson. God was saying that, though Elijah himself would not be so occupied, vengeance would indeed come in due time. Elijah really did not need to be told where and how to do a prophet's work. On the other hand, he did not know the answer as to retribution against Jezebel and Baal worship. Would God let this wicked person escape her due punishment? It had seemed so from the clear "no" to the tornado, earthquake and fire. God did see fit to set his mind at ease. There *would* be punishment, but

136

in His own time and way. Elijah would not bring it, but others would. Elijah would have some part, however, in at least anointing to office those who would effect it. Even this would be only representatively in the case of two, as Elijah would learn in due time. Elisha and Elisha's servant were actually to anoint Hazael and Jehu respectively.

1. Fulfillment of the Assignments

Elijah himself anointed only Elisha. He did this as soon as he returned to the land, going directly to Abel-meholah[15] where Elisha lived. Elisha then accompanied him for his remaining years of ministry. During this time Ahab died (1 Kings 22:37), Ahaziah reigned two years and died (1 Kings 22:51; 2 Kings 1:17) and Jehoram began to rule (2 Kings 3:1-3). Jehoram ruled a total of twelve years or about eleven years after Elijah's death. It was only then that a second of the anointings was possible, with Elisha sending "one of the sons of the prophets" to anoint Jehu to replace Jehoram (2 Kings 9:1-10).[16] A total of about twenty-one years had passed since God's instructions. The third anointing, that of Hazael over Syria, was effected by Elisha personally about one year prior to that of Jehu, approximately twenty years after Mount Horeb (2 Kings 8:7-15, 28, 29).

2. Fulfillment of the Vengeance

This means that for about twenty years the "still small voice" method of patience continued as God's manner of dealing with the wicked court. Elijah with Elisha, and then Elisha alone, went through the land simply preaching and encouraging as the Baal program remained in power. Perhaps the two prophets often shook their heads puzzling over God's longsuffering. But God was giving the royal family and the people full opportunity to repent if they would. However, the twenty years of patience finally ran out, and God's clock of justice struck.

137

Jehu swept across the Jordan from Ramoth-gilead, where he had been anointed, to Jezreel where Jehoram was recovering from a wound. The young men who had anointed him had brought orders: "And thou shalt smite the house of Ahab thy master, . . . avenge the blood of . . . the prophets . . . at the hand of Jezebel" (2 Kings 9:7). He did just that. He first killed Jehoram[17] and Jehoram's cousin, Ahaziah, then king of Judah visiting from Jerusalem. Jezebel, looking from an upper palace window, was cast down at his command and died and dogs ate her flesh. Ahab's seventy sons in Samaria were beheaded there by the city's frightened leaders, who then sent their heads to Jehu in Jezreel in a gesture of transferred allegiance. Jehu himself slew "all that remained of the house of Ahab in Jezreel, and all his great men, and his familiar friends, and his priests, until he left him none remaining" (2 Kings 10:11). Departing for Samaria, he met and killed forty-two "brethren of Ahaziah" (10:13, 14) coming to Jezreel to visit. Upon reaching the capital, "he smote all that remained unto Ahab in Samaria" (10:17). Finally he gathered into their temple and slew all the priests of Baal. When he had finished, God commended him (10:30). He had effected the promised and necessary retribution the tornado, earthquake and fire depicted to Elijah.

A year earlier, as noted, Hazael had been anointed king of Syria. When doing so, Elisha had wept and explained to Hazael: "Because I know the evil that thou wilt do unto the children of Israel: their strongholds wilt thou set on fire, and their young men wilt thou slay with the sword, and wilt dash in pieces their little ones, and rip up their women with child" (2 Kings 8:12).

Hazael had little to do in punishing the house of Ahab itself, for Jehu did all that was possible and necessary.[18] Clear implications exist that he did much to complete the punishment in respect to the country generally, which Jehu did not do.[19] One implication comes from Elisha's words just noted, that Hazael would work this extreme havoc in the land. He would not have predicted something that was not to come to pass. Evidently Elisha had been told by Elijah to carry out this anointing and something of the significance when he did.[20] Another comes from 2 Kings 13:3, 4 where it is said that God delivered the land "into the hand of Hazael king of Syria, and into the hand of Ben-hadad the son of Hazael, continually." At no other time in Israel's history is a similar degree of submission of Israel to Syria indicated. A third comes from 2 Kings 12:17, 18. Here Hazael, evidently now having Israel in complete subjection, pressed on even to Jerusalem and "took all the hallowed things that Jehoshaphat and Jehoram and Ahaziah, . . . kings of Judah, had dedicated." It is clear that Israel was terribly humiliated by this foreign ruler, the completion of what God had promised to Elijah on Mount Horeb.

God's hand of justice did fall; He did repay in His own time. It was hard for Elijah to understand the waiting. It had seemed to him that punishment was needed immediately, but God had seen it best to give time for repentance through the "still small voice" of preaching. However, that time of patience elapsed and God brought the retribution. This is a picture of God's way of working in this world. He is patient and longsuffering, giving abundant opportunity for repentance. He has His servants preaching the Word. He wants people to respond to the message, urging with tender invitation, yet few do. Most go their own way—proud, self-sufficient, loving their sin. God continues to be patient. However, this does not mean that He overlooks the sin. He notes it and in due time will speak in His wrath regarding it, if repentance is not forthcoming. He spoke in the form of the flood in the days of Noah. He spoke here most severely to Jezebel and Israel through two kings. He will speak to all men who reject the Savior in unending punishment in eternity to come. Vengeance does belong to God and He does repay. The warning of God must never be taken lightly.

Footnotes to Chapter Twelve:

[1]Here God gave the law to Moses; appeared to Moses in the burning bush, giving instructions for his return to Egypt (Exod. 3, 4); and, later, after Israel's defection with the golden calf, placed Moses in "a cleft of the rock" where he might view God's "back parts" as He passed by (Exod. 33:18-23).

[2]God may even have providentially directed his steps to the very cave where Moses had hidden as God passed by.

[3]*Supra*, p. 111.

[4]The word used (*qol*) is good for either "voice" or "sound." It is used also in the following verse and there clearly means a speaking voice, which could argue that it means the same here. If so, no indication is given of what was said. The message given in the following verse comes only after Elijah walks entirely out of the cave, and so should not be confused with whatever message may have been given here.

[5]Matthew 8:27. Cf. Mark 4:41; Luke 8:25.

[6]Mark 6:51, 52. Matthew 14:33 says significantly, "And they that were in the boat worshipped him, saying, Of a truth thou art the Son of God." Their amazement, then, even drew forth this worship and acclamation.

[7]Interestingly, God also impressed Israel with His great power in nature at Mount Horeb (Exod. 19:16-19).

[8]This lesson would not have been so meaningful for Elijah as it is for us. However, it would have shown him how greatly God wanted him back in service.

[9]This lesson was the most basic of the five, as noted earlier, *supra*, pp. 114, 115.

[10]This is not to say that God was not in this planning. He was, but this also was clearly the type of thing Elijah delighted in. Further, Elijah was mistaken in thinking that this big approach was all that mattered.

[11]*Supra*, pp. 114, 115.

[12]The nearest to something big came when he called down fire on the two companies of fifty sent by Ahaziah (2 Kings 1:1-16). However, this did not involve a general endeavor for revival, but was a way of personally impressing the king with Jehovah's authority.

[13]In keeping is God's characterization of preaching as "foolishness" in the eyes of the world (1 Cor. 1:21). Sacred history seldom shows God working swiftly. He used over six hundred years to fulfill

His promise to Abraham respecting a land and a people to dwell in it. He took eighty years to equip Moses for leadership when all the while the people suffered bondage.

[14]Jonah had a problem in leaving vengeance in God's hands. He complained that God did not bring vengeance on Nineveh as Jonah had predicted. Amazingly, he even objected that God was "a gracious God, and merciful, slow to anger, and abundant in lovingkindness . . ." (Jonah 4:2).

[15]Nelson Glueck identifies Abel-meholah with Tell el-Maqlub in the territory of Issachar. This means that Elijah had to travel well up the Jordan valley to find Elisha.

[16]Jehu was a captain in Jehoram's army. Being at Ramoth-gilead, he was not far from the scene of the battle in which Jehoram had recently been wounded (2 Kings 8:28).

[17]The record of these deeds is found in 2 Kings 9:14–10:30.

[18]Though Hazael was anointed a year prior to Jehu, still, being a foreign king, his affliction of Israel did not take form until during Jehu's reign. In that Jehu slew all Ahab's house, there was no more that Hazael could do in this respect, though he had, before this, at least wounded Jehoram in battle.

[19]Obviously Jehu, now Israel's king, was not interested in hurting his own country. This was the reason why it was necessary to involve also a foreign king if the vindication promised was to be effected fully.

[20]This confirms the fact that Elijah had caught the significance of these instructions back at Mount Horeb. This could be expected, of course, since God would not have told him these things if he would not have been able to understand.

Chapter Thirteen

BACK IN ISRAEL

Four brief, well-separated glimpses are given of Elijah's ministry after returning to Israel. The first, his call of Elisha, began the ministry; and the last, his own miraculous transport to Heaven, closed it. The second, his rebuke of King Ahab following Ahab's seizure of Naboth's vineyard, came perhaps after five years; and the third, his rebuke of the new king, Ahaziah, Ahab's son, preceded his transport by about one year. This means that there is not as continuous a narrative for the "still small voice" ministry as that we have thus far considered. The accounts included, however, give key reflection as to the conditions Elijah faced during this period and his manner of meeting them. They are significant too in the valuable lessons they present for our learning. They do not call for lengthy discussion and so may be treated together in this closing chapter.

Elisha's Call (1 Kings 19:19-21)

The first account, concerning Elisha's call, follows immediately in the text after the portion we have thus far discussed. Apparently Elijah went directly in obedience to God's instruction to call the young man, which means that he had him as a helper throughout his remaining years of ministry. We may be sure that they made a splendid team. Certainly the high tribute given to Elijah at the close of his life

142

was due in part to having had a good assistant. This is easy to believe too in view of the excellent ministry Elisha then continued for himself.

When Elijah found him, Elisha "was plowing, with twelve yoke of oxen before him, and he with the twelfth . . ." (v. 19). This shows that Elisha was a worker. He was hard at work when Elijah found him. God is not looking for lazy people, interested in an easy job. He calls workers who are ready to put forth real energy for Him. He was also of a well-to-do family. Twelve men and twenty-four animals laboring in one field speak of substantial capital and efficient organization. Elisha would be leaving an attractive future when he followed Elijah.

Elijah "cast his mantle upon" Elisha to indicate the call.[1] Elisha recognized the gesture and gave immediate response, asking only first to bid farewell to his parents. This suggests that Elisha had been prepared beforehand. He could hardly have made this decision so quickly otherwise. Somehow God had inclined his heart, burdened him with the sin of the people, and stirred him with the vision of a prophetic ministry. He was ready to obey whenever God might call. It must be that Elisha recognized Elijah from a previous contact and needed nothing more than this gesture to be convinced that this was that call.

God is looking for this kind of response. This is different from what Moses displayed when he argued long with God why he should not return to Egypt (Exod. 3, 4); or that Jonah gave when he fled in the opposite direction from where God had told him to go (Jonah 1:1-3). This is like Isaiah's response, who said, "Here am I; send me" (Isa. 6:8). It is a privilege to serve God. One should be ready and eager for the gracious invitation.

Was Elisha wrong in asking to bid farewell to his parents? Jesus said, "No man, having put his hand to the plow, and looking back, is fit for the kingdom of God" (Luke

143

9:62). He said this in reference to those making excuse for not following Him, among whom was one who wished to "bid farewell to them that" were at home (v. 61). The two instances are quite different, however. The man of whom Jesus spoke was making an excuse so as not to have to follow. Elisha was fully prepared to follow, but only wished to say good-bye. In this he was showing proper respect for his parents, which was altogether right. Accordingly, we do not hear Elijah extending any rebuke, but saying, "Go back again" (v. 20). Elijah's continuing words, "For what have I done to thee?" mean only that Elijah had not by this action put any constraint on Elisha; the decision was his alone.

It should be noticed too that Elisha completely severed home ties when he left. He killed the oxen with which he had been plowing and broke up his plow for fuel. The immediate reason was to provide meat for a farewell feast with his family and friends, but no one could have missed the added significance. Elisha was cutting off old ties entirely. He would have no equipment with which to work if he should ever return home again. He meant business in his new decision. This sort of decisiveness is important for the one who obeys the call of God. It tells others of one's own sincerity, as here. It also puts away unnecessary temptation to return should one later feel so inclined. When God calls, it is final. Our response should be equally final.

Rebuke of Ahab (1 Kings 21:1-29)

The story of Elijah's rebuke of Ahab for seizing Naboth's vineyard tells of what was probably the only contact between these two persons following the Mount Carmel contest. No intimation is found that there was any other, and Ahab's first words this time, "Hast thou found me, O mine enemy?" (v. 20), suggest that no meeting had preceded this at least. The story is significant too in showing the manner

144

of Ahab and Jezebel's continuing rule over Israel, and especially of Jezebel's ruthless ways in achieving her ends.

A few years had elapsed since Elisha's call.[2] The effects of the great famine had disappeared. Crops were growing and the country was reasonably prosperous once again. Vineyards like Naboth's were attractive and his became the object of Ahab's desire in the story. People would have settled themselves under the strong domination of the royal family once more, with Baal worship being as strong as ever. For some reason Jezebel had chosen to leave Elijah alone since his return. She likely had kept close check on his activities; but perhaps, due to his pursuing a different course of action than before, and also not wanting to re-inflame old wounds by unnecessary violence, she had let him carry on this quiet type of ministry quite unmolested.

Elijah's involvement in the story comes only at its close. Ahab had desired a vineyard close to his Jezreel palace. It belonged to Naboth, who refused on legal grounds[3] to sell it to the king. Jezebel, seeing Ahab's displeasure, arranged for an unjust trial and death sentence for Naboth,[4] and so made the vineyard available to Ahab.[5] When he went to occupy it, Elijah met him and administered the rebuke (21:17-26).

The rebuke was strong, consisting mainly of a description of impending calamity for Ahab's house. We may believe that Ahab was quite astonished. The last time he had seen Elijah, the prophet had favored him by providing himself as a personal escort through pelting rain. Moreover, since that time Elijah had displayed quite normal fears in running from the queen. He apparently was vincible after all. But suddenly here he was again, and without any sign of weakness now. He was bringing severe rebuke and predicting destruction for the king's entire household.

Elijah's opening words were, "Hast thou killed, and also taken possession?" (v. 19). Ahab could not mistake the incident of which the prophet spoke, for Ahab was even then in the act of taking possession of Naboth's vineyard. The next words began the prediction of calamity: ". . . In the place where dogs licked the blood of Naboth shall dogs lick thy blood, even thine." Naboth had died in Jezreel, and so this prediction was not fulfilled in every detail in that Ahab died in Samaria; but dogs did lick his blood from his chariot (22:38). This permitted change from the prediction was granted in view of Ahab's contrition (21:27-29). Elijah's words were fulfilled on this count, however, with Ahab's son, Jehoram (2 Kings 9:25, 26).

At this point, Ahab interrupted with the question noted above, "Hast thou found me, O mine enemy?" This was an effort at retaliation. Elijah was not his enemy. He had proved that on Mount Carmel. If the king could so categorize him, his own conscience might ease itself by discounting much that such an one would say. It might also distract the prophet from continuing these dire predictions. This last it did not do, for Elijah pressed on unmercifully.

Not only Ahab himself, but also his sons, all of them, would experience like fate; even as with the houses of both Jeroboam (1 Kings 15:25-30) and Baasha (1 Kings 16:8-13) years before (vv. 21, 22). As for Jezebel, the dogs would eat her "by the rampart of Jezreel" (1 Kings 21:23). Further, in general terms, "Him that dieth of Ahab in the city the dogs" would eat; "and him that dieth in the field . . . the birds of the heavens" would eat (v. 24).

What these somber words amounted to was an explicit voicing of the implications God had set forth on Mount Horeb, as seen in the preceding chapter. Symbol only had been employed then in the form of predicted anointings of two kings. Here Elijah was making very plain to the king what had been intended, which shows further that Elijah had understood. The tornado, earthquake and fire were in truth to be used in due time. The house of Ahab and Jezebel was to experience utter destruction.

As a further indication of patience on God's part, however, it should be noticed that Elijah's message constituted a warning in view of which Ahab could profit if he chose. God might have just let the punishment fall, but He thus provided gracious warning. And Ahab did repent. "He rent his clothes, and put sackcloth upon his flesh, and fasted, and lay in sackcloth, and went softly" (v. 27). No indication is made that Jezebel did this, but Ahab did.[6] The description suggests a repentance of considerable degree too. It was not lasting, however, as witnessed by his soon dependence on false prophets and imprisonment of Micaiah (1 Kings 22). But for what it was, God gave respite. Jehovah did not "bring the evil in his days; but in his son's day" (v. 29).

This does not mean that God changed His mind. He did not suddenly switch from Ahab to Jehoram. The symbolism back on Mount Horeb had already indicated that Jehu would be the one to bring the calamity; and his time to do this would be at the close of Jehoram's rule, not Ahab's. God simply had anticipated this contrition on Ahab's part in assigning the calamity as He did. On the other hand, it will not do either to say that Ahab's repentance was immaterial. It was material and very necessary on Ahab's part. In fact, one may say that had Ahab not repented, the punishment would have come on him. God, knowing all things, knew he would repent and gave His prediction to Elijah accordingly several years before.[7]

We should understand that Ahab's repentance was not repentance unto salvation. There is no indication that Ahab ever did repent to this degree. Still God honored it. He postponed the punishment to the day of his son, who did not so repent. God did similarly in respect to the people of Nineveh who repented at the preaching of Jonah (Jonah 3:5-10). As a result, God did not destroy the city. God always honors repentance, providing it is sincere. The highest type of repentance is from sin itself, and not merely from some sinful act, and then God can honor by impartation of new life in salvation. But wherever there is repentance of any kind, even if only temporary and in respect to one action, God recognizes it and provides appropriate respite. This respite always corresponds to the degree and type of repentance. Anything other than repentance unto salvation results only in some earthly benefit, but nonetheless is still very real. Let no man say that God is unjust or unkind. God punishes only because man persists unrepentingly in his sin.

Rebuke of Ahaziah (2 Kings 1:1-18)

The third account is from the days of Ahab's son and successor, Ahaziah. He ruled only two years and the incident comes at the close of that time, involving, in fact, the prediction of his death. The occasion gives a picture of this wicked man's reign and tells of his one contact with Elijah.

Ahaziah had met with an accident, falling "through the lattice in his upper chamber . . ." (2 Kings 1:2).[8] He sent messengers to inquire of Baal-zebub,[9] god of the city of Ekron, as to possible recovery. The "angel of Jehovah" told Elijah to intercept the messengers, give rebuke to the king through them for seeking information from this false god and predict Ahaziah's death. When Ahaziah received this report, recognizing Elijah's identity from the description of the messengers,[10] he sent fifty men to bring Elijah to the capital. Elijah called destroying fire down from Heaven upon this company and then upon another sent by Ahaziah before a third group came humbly entreating for their lives. With them the prophet finally went to see the king.

Elijah has been criticized for this severe action relative to the one hundred men thus killed. They were only carrying out orders, so why take their lives? However, they represented a Jehovah-defying king who needed strong rebuke, and a measure this severe was necessary to make rebuke effective. Ahaziah was pursuing his mother's footsteps–following Baal, not Jehovah. Here he was sending outside Israel,[11] to the Philistine city of Ekron, for desired revelation. Reprimand, strongly given, was in order. Then the men of these two companies were themselves arrogant before Jehovah's prophet. They cried, "O man of God, the king hath said, Come down" (v. 9). This showed little respect for one who was the prophet of God. They thought themselves to be so much in charge that Elijah should listen, or else. But Elijah, representing the true God, could not be ordered in this fashion. Jehovah was supreme in the land, not Baal. These men must be made to realize this, as well as the king and others who would later learn what happened. So let fire fall from Heaven. It had signified Who was the true God in Ahab's day; it would again now in Ahaziah's.

It was only when the third company did come humbly that Elijah was permitted to acquiesce to the request. God recognizes and extends grace to the contrite, but not to the proud. This is always true. The sinner can only be saved when he humbles himself in accepting Christ as Lord and Savior. The Christian can only be blessed as he walks humbly in his day by day conduct. Humility is necessary for it reflects the reality of man's dependence. God is supreme and absolute; man is finite and contingent. Man lives only because God maintains him. This basic truth is recognized in humility. Accordingly, God can bring blessing only where it is found, as illustrated so graphically in this account.

Elijah's message to Ahaziah upon arriving was brief and only repeated what had already been said through the first messengers: ". . . Forasmuch as thou hast sent messengers to inquire of Baal-zebub, the god of Ekron, is it because there is no God in Israel to inquire of his word? therefore thou shalt not come down from the bed whither thou art gone up, but shalt surely die" (v. 16). He gave rebuke for sending to this foreign deity, which on Ahaziah's part had been tantamount to saying that Israel's God was inadequate. He

149

also predicted the king's death, indicating that this would be the king's punishment for such action.

God takes note of all sin. His patience should never be confused with His acquiescence. This sin of Ahaziah's was particularly serious because he, as king, would be influencing others in it. Leadership always involves increased responsibility. If he should not be stopped and punished, others learning of it would be encouraged to follow suit. Jehovah would be further dishonored and Baal made to grow in prominence. God could not have this and took the action we have observed.

Elijah's prediction came true, as verse 17 states. Ahaziah died. This means that this was another instance when God gave warning ahead of time that a man might repent if he would. We have just seen this with Ahab, and he did profit. Ahaziah did not. He did not repent and the warning was carried out as given. God regularly gives warning before punishment. He gave it through Noah for a hundred and twenty years before the great flood; and through prophets to Israel many times before permitting the captivity. He gives it to the world today through His written Word. Eternal punishment impends for all who reject the Savior. God warns that men might heed. How heartrending that so many do not, even as Ahaziah.

Miraculous Home-going (2 Kings 2:1-15)

The final account concerns Elijah's unique and honored departure for Heaven. He did not die but was specially transported.

God told Elijah ahead of time that his home-going would be unique. Also, Elisha and the "sons of the prophets" (v. 3) were informed. These "sons of the prophets" were training prophets, in schools which Elijah likely had revived from the former days of Samuel.[12] Elijah did not know that these others had been told. Proceeding on a final visit to the

150

schools, Elijah urged Elisha three times, first at Gilgal and then at the schools in both Bethel and Jericho, not to accompany him, but Elisha persisted. At both schools the training prophets told Elisha that they knew of Elijah's impending departure and wondered if Elisha did. Elisha said he did and asked them not to speak further of the matter, apparently not wanting Elijah to learn that others knew. Elisha then continued with Elijah, crossing the Jordan which separated before them, and walked on to the place of the departure, where God caught Elijah "up by a whirlwind into heaven" (2:11).

Several observations are called for in view of unusual features in the story. Most important is the fact that in this special transportation God was honoring His prophet for fine service, as has been observed.[13] Elijah had been reprimanded severely at Mount Horeb; but after the intervening years of excellent ministry, he heard this "Well done, thou good and faithful servant." He needed to know of it ahead of time so as to walk to the place where it would be effected. Perhaps also God saw it fitting that he have this source of satisfaction during his closing hours on earth.

Elisha and the training prophets were informed of this impending honor because of the benefit they also would receive in simply knowing of it. Their individual faith would be strengthened for their own days of service to come as they would see an actual fulfillment of a promised miracle; and they would be encouraged to personal faithfulness as they witnessed the honor God was willing to bestow on a prophet for fine service.

Elijah urged Elisha not to accompany him because he wished to experience this honor alone. He looked at it as a precious, intimate climax to his life. He did not know that Elisha knew of it and thus felt that no disservice to him was involved. In fact, he may have believed it better that Elisha not know lest he compare this experience with that of others and later with his own.

Elisha recognized how much this time meant to his master and why he should want to experience it alone, and so was careful himself, and in warning the training prophets, not to let Elijah know that the knowledge was shared. Elijah had Elisha's interest in mind, and Elisha Elijah's. Elisha wished his master to enjoy this grand experience to the fullest extent.

Elisha also had been given to know that he should himself witness this event. We may believe that God either had told him directly or else implied it in the way in which He had informed him ahead of time regarding it. For actually to see the fulfillment would serve to impress its reality on his mind. It would be a stabilizing and encouraging memory all his life. He should insist on staying with Elijah, but without letting him know that he knew.

In view of this occurrence being so unusual, but yet with all factors having a very meaningful place, God's words to Isaiah come to mind: "For my thoughts are not your thoughts, neither are your ways my ways, saith Jehovah" (Isa. 55:8). This was God's way of bringing the ministry of one of His faithful servants to a close, while at the same time honoring him and giving reasons for encouragement to others. It was in truth a way of which no man would have thought. It took God's wisdom to see the many benefits that would result. He knew the type of ministry that lay before both Elisha and these training young men, and how this memorable experience could be just the thing to spur them on and provide encouragement in days of difficulty. God's ways are always best. They often differ from what we would do in our limited perception, but He knows best. He sees all and works all for good to those who love Him (Rom. 8:28).

When Elijah and Elisha reached the Jordan, Elijah

struck the water with his mantle[14] and the waters divided to make a dry path.[15] People normally crossed the Jordan at shallow fording places, and certainly Elijah usually did too. The reason for dividing it this time was again to provide a faith lesson for both Elisha and the training prophets. The statement in verse 7 is significant: "Fifty men of the sons of the prophets" watched from a distance. Elijah wanted them to see the waters divide. In their schools they had heard of God's miraculous works, but probably had seen few if any. Here they would as Elijah left them. Elisha could also profit from a fresh impression of God's power at this crucial moment. Challenge would be provided for him too when he soon would return and stand on these same banks and demand that the waters act for him in similar fashion.

After crossing the Jordan, Elijah at last asked what he could do for Elisha before leaving him. Apparently he had finally discerned that the younger man had somehow come to know of what was to occur. Elisha asked for "a double portion of" Elijah's spirit, meaning the portion of the eldest son in an inheritance.[16] He desired to be recognized by Elijah as his eldest "son" among prophets of the day.

Elijah would have recognized readily the propriety of the request, for Elisha had been his close attendant and companion for several years. He would also have felt great admiration for Elisha in making it. Elisha was not asking for a physical provision, some material gift or possession. He was asking to be endowed with power by God's Spirit. So often material things loom large in life's evaluation and people are too strongly attracted to them. But Elisha wanted the same power that he had seen working through his master. He wanted to follow in the same footsteps; he wanted to do the same work. This was not merely romantic dreaming. Elisha knew the price involved. He had been with Elijah too long not to know this. He had heard of Elijah's earlier trials with the royal court, and how many the two of them had experienced together we can only guess. Apparently price was unimportant to this dedicated servant. He wanted to be used, empowered and filled with God's Spirit to continue the work of Elijah.

One of the greatest needs in God's work in any day is to have this kind of dedication on the part of young people looking forward to His service. Too often the "yes" of dedication is the expression only of a romantic spirit which turns to "no" when hardship is encountered. God wants true dedication, a willingness to do real work. This means to be empowered by God's Spirit and daily filled for victorious service. As each generation lays its task aside, a new one must take it up. Moses had his Joshua, Elijah his Elisha, Paul his Timothy. Workers are needed to carry on the task that some must lay down today.

Elijah could not voice all he felt in response to Elisha. He simply said that he had asked "a hard thing," by which he meant that he, Elijah, could not grant it of himself. To give God's Spirit to Elisha was beyond his control. Continuing to say that if Elisha saw him depart the request would be granted, Elijah was really committing the matter to God. If God should so effect the transportation that Elisha could witness it, then Elisha could know that the petition had been granted. Elisha kept close watch, and God did effect the departure so that he could see. With the request so admirable, Elijah could have guessed that God would honor it; but there was reason for Elisha's mind to be turned away from Elijah to God, in Whom alone lay the right and power. He, Elisha, must not think too highly of his departing master. Only God could grant the endowment of the Spirit.

The transportation is described as follows: "There appeared a chariot of fire, and horses of fire, which parted them both asunder; and Elijah went up by a whirlwind into heaven" (v. 11). This does not actually say that Elijah departed in the chariot. A chariot and horses are mentioned, but Elijah ascended "by a whirlwind." Likely the two were in some sense identical, however, with the wind perhaps having the appearance of a chariot and horses.[17] The details are really unimportant. The matter of significance is that the prophet was taken to Heaven without passing the normal portals of death.

Elisha, seeing him go, cried, "My father, my father, the chariots of Israel and the horsemen thereof" (v. 12). Elijah had been Elisha's spiritual father in having both called and taught him. Elisha gave vocal recognition of this treasured fact. He probably could not express enough how glad he was that this had been so. His life had been greatly changed because of Elijah.

Elijah had been Israel's chariot and horsemen—here used symbolically for strength and protection—in having long provided a strong defense for the kingdom through prayer, counsel and warning. This had been true though the king had little realized or appreciated it. God alone knew the extent of Israel's strength against economic poverty and military aggression during the previous ten years which was due to Elijah's work and intercession. Elisha's words imply that he had spent hours in prayer to this end, as well as ministering orally to hundreds, so that God's blessing had been upon the country. Elisha had knowledge of this because of his daily contact with the great prophet, and here gave due recognition.

It is no reason for Christians to be proud, but it is true that today nations also have much for which to thank God's people. History shows that prosperity and cultural advances have followed the gospel. In accordance with the number of its Christians and the earnestness of their ministry and prayer is the blessing of any community and nation. Every Christian has a major responsibility in praying for his country.

Elijah's mantle, with which he had parted the Jordan

shortly before, fell from his shoulders as he was caught upward; and Elisha, taking it as symbolic of the answer to his request, directly appropriated it for himself. Then he put it to quick use. Standing again at the bank of the Jordan, he spoke like Elijah and struck the waters once more. Would the waters divide for him? This was an important moment for Elisha. He had asked for spiritual endowment, and this would prove the granting of the request. The extent of his future ministry hinged upon what would happen. We may be sure that his delight was great as he saw the waters divide as they had before. He had been empowered. God had answered his prayer. He could take up the ministry that Elijah had laid down.

It is not our task to follow Elisha in this ministry. Our concern has been with Elijah. We have seen this great prophet stand courageously in a day of extreme declension. We have seen him stumble and then rise again under God's tender ministration. We have seen him train one to take his place. The manner in which Elisha filled that place would have made the teacher glad.

As a closing note, let us consider ourselves, now having made this study, to have been taught by this great man. The need is for us, like Elisha, to take up his mantle in our day and continue the vital task. The time is different and the conditions have changed, but the basic need is the same. Men need to be turned from their sin to God and prompted to place their faith in Him. Let us give ourselves to the task and acquit ourselves well as Elishas of the present day.

Footnotes to Chapter Thirteen:

[1]The mantle (*'addereth*) seems to have varied in kind. The word sometimes is used for a costly garment (Josh. 7:21, 24), such as worn by a king (Jonah 3:6). But Elijah's mantle certainly was not this costly. It must have been easily taken off so as to be cast quickly on Elisha, and later, when Elijah was taken to Heaven, to fall behind as he departed.

[2]At least two battles, likely no less than a year apart, had tran-

spired (1 Kings 20), and these could not have occurred soon after the famine either, for both countries needed to recuperate. Perhaps as much as five years had elapsed.

[3]Naboth spoke of this property as a part to the inheritance of his fathers, and the law forbade its sale (Lev. 25:23-28; Num. 36:7).

[4]Second Kings 9:26 indicates also that Naboth's sons were executed, which was necessary so that there would be no heirs.

[5]The extent of Jezebel's control is here revealed. When a ruler can demand courts to decide unjustly to meet their wishes, then all manner of injustice becomes possible.

[6]This fact again shows a marked difference between Ahab and his queen. She had been the leader in the Baal program from the start and would not repent here. Verse 25 states directly that she had stirred him up in his working wickedness.

[7]This is not to imply that God bases His actions on mere foreknowledge, as though man could actually determine the nature of God's actions; but only to show factors that did enter God's own sovereign decision.

[8]The word translated "lattice" (sebakah) is often translated "network" in connection with the temple construction (1 Kings 7:17, 18, 20, 41, 42). It was probably something like a window screen through which the king fell, perhaps even to the ground some distance below.

[9]The name Baal-zebub means "lord of flies." It is conjectured that this god was symbolized as a fly and reputed to have great predictive power.

[10]Very likely Ahaziah had learned of Elijah while a prince in the palace, perhaps even having seen him out on Mount Carmel the day of the contest. Evidently Elijah always wore similar clothing so that Ahaziah could recognize him by the description given: "A hairy man, and girt with a girdle of leather about his loins."

[11]Ekron had been a major Philistine city near the Israelite border. In Samuel's day it became Israelite property (1 Sam. 7:14), but by Saul's reign it had returned to the Philistines (1 Sam. 17:52) and apparently remained so (Amos 1:8) for many years, including this time of Elijah's activity.

[12]Nearly two hundred years had passed since Samuel and no mention is made during this time of these schools continuing. Elijah likely started them again in view of the great spiritual darkness and need for true prophets, especially in the northern kingdom.

[13]Supra, pp. 133, 134.

[14]Same garment ('addereth) that Elijah cast on Elisha at his call and which Elisha, just a few hours later, again used to part the Jordan.

¹⁵This act was particularly impressive for it carried historical significance: Israel had crossed similarly years before.

¹⁶Cf. Deuteronomy 21:17. The idea that Elisha received twice as much power as Elijah is not valid. Though more miracles of Elisha are recorded, this does not mean that he performed more. And none excelled in power such as raising the widow's son, calling down fire, stopping and starting rain, etc. Also, Elijah received higher honor from God than Elisha; *supra,* p. 9.

¹⁷It may be pertinent too that Elisha later (2 Kings 6:17) saw God's protective angels in the form of "horses and chariots." This chariot with horses may have represented God's angel sent to provide this special transportation device, which would have sped skyward in the "whirlwind." The word for wind, *se'arah,* means a storm which shakes violently. It was not a general storm here but a concentrated wind like a "whirlwind."

Made in the USA
Coppell, TX
08 November 2022

86004789R00089